What's Inside

Alphabet Activities presents lessons that help emerging readers and writers practice letter-sound associations while they learn and use computer drawing and keyboarding tools.

Each lesson in *Alphabet Activities* has been successfully used with kindergarten and first-grade students in a class setting. Step-by-step directions make the lessons easy to use by teachers of all levels of computer expertise.

Alphabet Activities is divided into four sections.

Your Friendly User Manual pages 2–15

Here you will find ideas on how to use the activities, helpful computer tips, suggestions for introducing the computer to your students, and picture and word cards that present computer icons and vocabulary.

Individual-Letter Activities pages 16–67

This section contains a two-page lesson for each letter:

- The first page gives step-by-step teacher directions, lesson extensions, and literature connections.
- The second page provides simplified student directions with picture guides that can be displayed at the computer to help students work independently.

Multiple-Letter Activities pages 68–77

Here are five fun activities to reinforce multiple-letter recognition and provide alphabet practice.

Teaching Aids pages 78–80

Aids include a computer skills checklist, an activity checklist, and a parent letter to use when you send home an alphabet project.

How to Use Alphabet Activities

- While the activities in this guide are presented in alphabetical order, they may be used in any order. Simply check the use of tools in the activity to make sure that you are not introducing too many new tools in one lesson.

    For example:

    The lesson for the letter A requires use of the drawing tool, fill tool, and copy and paste. The lesson for the letter L uses only the paint tool.

  Cutting and pasting requires following multistep directions. Make sure your students are ready before you expect them to do this independently. (See "Creating a Template" on page 4 for an easy alternative.)

- The activities suggested in this book are not program specific. They can be used with any computer program that includes drawing and word-processing tools (Kid Pix Studio®, KidWorks®, and others). Directions will be given in generic terminology, but you will need to be familiar with the specific terms for the program you are using.
- The activities can be done on a single computer in the classroom, first as a demonstration, and then rotating individual students through a center; or in a computer lab with all students working simultaneously. If students are working independently, reproduce the step-by-step picture directions for a specific lesson, and post them by the computer to help students remember their job.
- Refer to the Literature Connections provided with each activity for suggested trade books that enhance the computer lesson.

    For example:

    When you introduce Fancy Fish, read Lois Ehlert's *Fish Eyes.* Discuss the different shapes and decorations that the author uses to make her fish more interesting.

- Individual projects can be...

printed see pages 4 and 5	saved in a computer file see page 5	used in a class slide show see page 6	simply erased

Computer Etiquette

Develop some general expectations with your students for computer use.

Don't Let the Computer Intimidate You

- Practice the lesson or project before instructing students. Make sure that you are comfortable with the steps from beginning to end.
- Do your initial instruction with students gathered around as you demonstrate the steps. As students use the same tools in several activities, ask lots of questions and let the students guide you through the steps that they are familiar with. Modify activities, if necessary, so that you limit the new steps and procedures introduced at a single session.
- If you are working with a whole class, hook your computer monitor to your classroom television with a video out cable so that students can see more easily. (Some additional hardware may be necessary.)

> If something unexpected occurs, don't be afraid to say, "I don't know what happened. Let's try again."

Creating a Template

When young students first begin using the computer, you may want to create a template and then have each student work with that template.

Suppose you want to use the activity "A Row of Apples" with a group of kindergarten students near the beginning of the year. Cutting and pasting with computer tools may require too many steps for your students. Modify the lesson by creating a template.

Before the activity:

1. Draw an apple.
2. Copy and paste apples to make a row of apples.
3. Save the row of apples (the template) on your computer.

To do the activity with students:

For one computer—Open the saved template and have students create their patterns with colors and details.

For more than one computer—Copy the template onto the computers to be used. Open the saved template on the different machines and have students create their patterns.

Screen Snapshots

When you develop your own activities, illustrate your directions with a series of screen snapshots (or print screens). Print screen procedures are different on a Mac than on a PC. Check the manual for how to do a print screen on your computer.

Some Thoughts on Printing

Reasons to print:

Young students love to print out their work. Their work becomes real when they can hold it in their hands.

Printing can also:

- **improve communication with parents**
- **reinforce learning as students explain their activities**
- **serve as basis for class books, displays, and bulletin boards**

Waiting while it prints:

In a situation where a number of computers use the available printers, help students to understand why printing can be slow.

"We have 25 computers connected to three printers. The computers stand in line for the printer just like we stand in line to get a drink at the drinking fountain. Sometimes the computers stand in a long line, and sometimes the line is short."

Criteria for printing:

Develop simple printing guidelines with your students.

Ask before you print.

Print only your best work!

Timely tips:

- Printing small is faster than printing regular size. Prints very often are charming in miniature.
- If you want to save ink and print full size, have students eliminate background color and fill steps. They can use the printed image as a coloring page and use markers or crayons to finish the activity.
- A lab of computers connected to a single printer is slow. It may be better to save students' work and print when the lab is empty.

Saving Student Work

If you want to save student work, you have several choices:

- Save on your hard drive.

  You can create a folder for individual projects on the hard drive of your computer and save all the student projects to that folder. You can open the project whenever you want so the work is not lost.

- Save on a disk.

  Format a disk for student work. Create a folder on the disk and save student projects to that folder. You will be able to retrieve the projects from the disk on any computer.

- Save on the network.

  If your computer is networked to a school server, create a class work folder on the server. Log on and save student work into the folder. Then you can access the work from any computer on the network.

Creating a Slide Show Using Student Work

A slide show is a multimedia presentation. It can be presented in story form or simply as a visual "list" of projects.

Steps to follow*:

1. Open the slide show tool in your program.
2. Choose a saved picture.
3. Put the saved picture in the first frame of the slide show.
4. Continue to put saved pictures in order.
5. Choose the musical transition you would like and the time each slide should remain on the screen.
6. Add recorded descriptions or sound effects.
7. Save your show.
8. Play the show and enjoy it. (Select the looped feature to see it play again and again without stopping.)

* Check the manual for the program you are using for any variation from the procedure given here.

Getting Your Students Started on the Computer

If your students are not familiar with the use of the computer as a tool for learning, introduce the computer using the suggestions on pages 8–10 before doing the letter activities in the book.

Learning that the computer is a tool:

Here is a sample scenario of how an introductory lesson might proceed:

"What do you use when you want to pound a nail into a wall?"
(a hammer)

"What do you use when you want to cut a board into two pieces?"
(a saw)

"What do you use when you want to sharpen your pencil?"
(a pencil sharpener)

"What do you use when you want to mow your lawn?"
(a lawn mower)

"Does anyone know a word that we use to describe all of these special things?"
("That's right - TOOLS - tools help us to do our work.")

"We have a special tool in our room that helps us to do our school work. Can anyone guess what it is? Right! It's a computer. The computer helps us draw, write, find information, and practice the things that we are learning. The computer is a tool that you will use all through your life, so it is important to learn how to use it well.

"If you didn't know how to use a hammer, you might not be able to pound that nail into the wall. But if your dad or mom or brother or sister taught you how to hold the hammer and how to hit the nail, could you take care of that nail?

"If you don't know how to use a computer, you will not be able to do the work you need to do. So we'll work here at school to learn how to use each part of the computer. Then, we'll practice so that we'll all be able to use the computer to help us do our work more efficiently."

Introducing the parts of a computer:

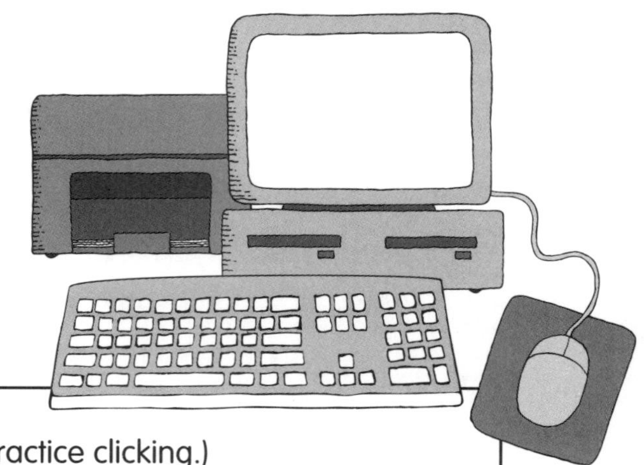

Gather students around an actual computer as you introduce its parts. On page 10 you will find a diagram showing the parts of a computer. This chart may be pasted beside your computer(s) or reproduced for individual students.

Here is a sample script for introducing parts of a computer to young learners:

The mouse:

(Have a bucket of "mice" available for students to practice clicking.)

"This is the mouse. Can anyone guess why someone named this part of the computer a mouse? See its long tail? The mouse's tail hooks to the computer. We use the mouse to tell the computer what we want it to do."

"We move the mouse on this special pad called a mouse pad. When we move the mouse, it moves the line or arrow in the computer. When we push down on the top of the mouse it's called clicking the mouse. Can you hear the little click the mouse makes when I push down on the top? Try clicking your own mouse. Listen for the sound. Sometimes we push twice on the mouse. That's called a double-click. Click-Click. Try a double-click on your mouse. Lots of times we tell the computer what to do by clicking the mouse."

The monitor:

"The monitor of a computer is like the screen of a television. It's where we see what is happening."

The keyboard:

"The keyboard of a computer is like a typewriter. It has all the letters of the alphabet and all the numbers. We can push the keys and the letters and numbers will show up on the screen of the monitor. Sometimes we tap keys on the keyboard to tell the computer what we want it to do."

The CPU:

"The CPU is the "brain" of the computer. This is where the parts and information that tell the computer how to work are found."

Computer Vocabulary Cards

Pages 12–15 provide 24 word and picture cards for vocabulary frequently used in the lessons in this book. The picture guides used will be similar, but not identical, to the icons used by your program. Periodic sessions with these cards will help your students to be comfortable with the student directions for the lessons and to develop a basic computer reading vocabulary.

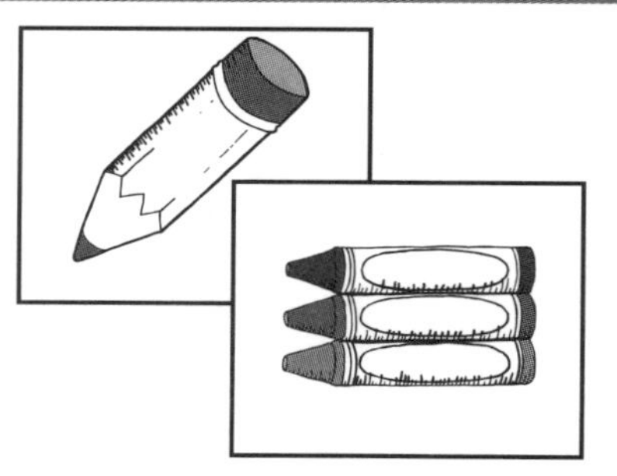

Introducing the Drawing Tools

Pose this question to students: "If you wanted to make a picture, what would you use?"
(crayons, pencil, paper, paint, scissors, paste)

"Inside my computer I have all of those things ready to use. I keep them in a program called *(name of program that you use).*"

Opening the Program

- For students who have never used the computer, have the program open for them the first few times they use it.
- Depending on your situation, you may want to store the program on the hard drive, the desktop, or a launcher. Wherever you put the program, students can identify it more easily if there is a distinctive icon on the program folder.

Putting an icon on the program folder using a Macintosh:

1. Open the program and find a folder with a picture that you want to use as the identifying icon. Click on the folder.
2. Go to File—Get Info.
3. Click on the picture.
4. Go to Edit—Copy.
5. Return to the program folder.
6. Click on the program.
7. Go to File—Get Info.
8. Click on the current icon for the program.
9. Go to Edit—Paste.
10. Save the program folder with its new icon on the desktop or launcher for easy access.

Creating a shortcut to the program using a PC:

1. Right click the mouse on the desktop.
2. Choose New from the pull-down menu.
3. Choose Shortcut.
4. Choose Browse.
5. Select the program by double clicking.
6. Click Next.
7. Change the program name if you like.
8. Click Finish. The icon for the program will be on the desktop.

- Develop a procedure for opening and closing the program you will use. Model and practice the procedure with your students several times. Soon your students will be opening and closing the program independently.

Note: Reproduce this chart showing the parts of a computer for your classroom.

My Computer

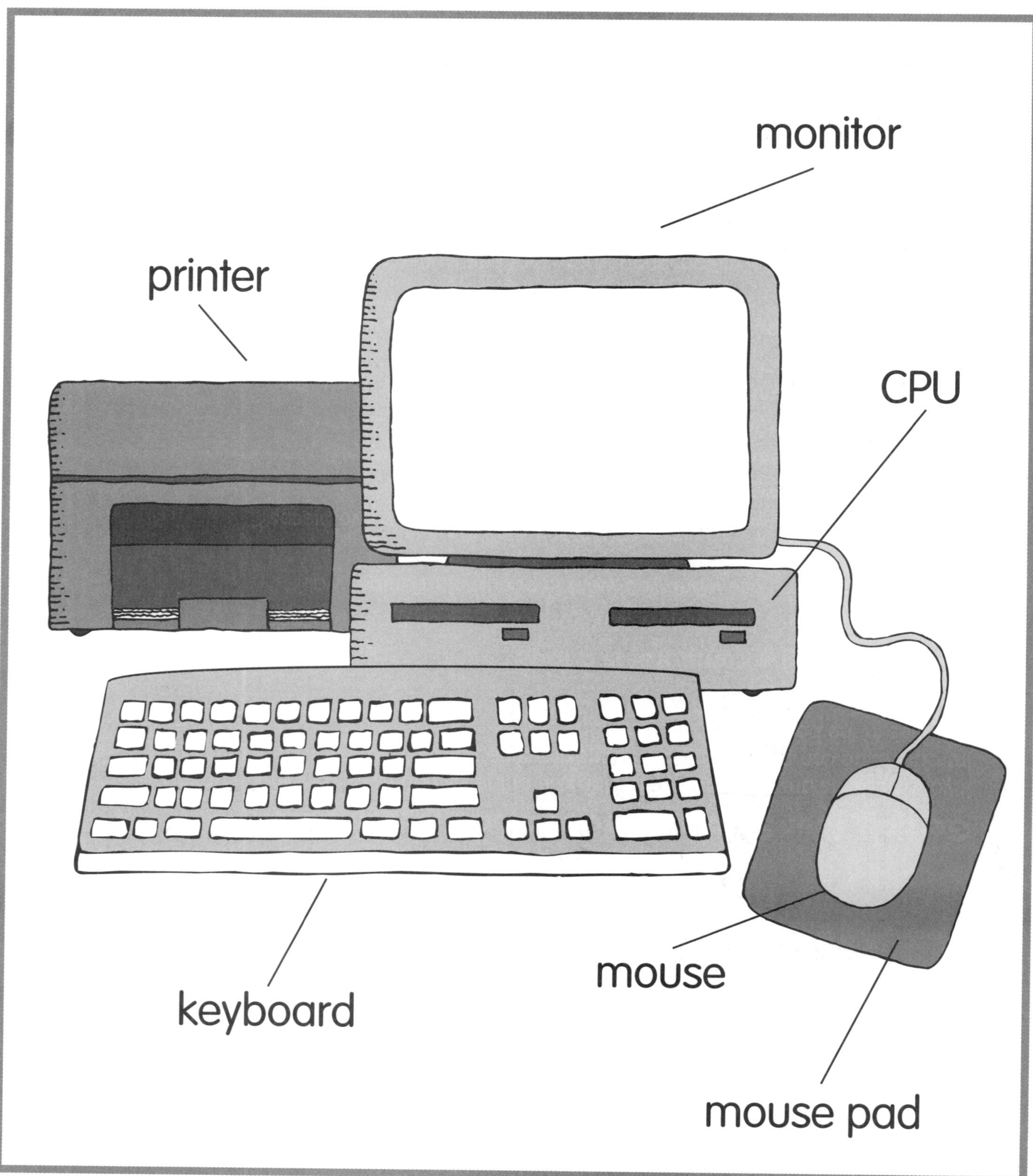

I use the computer to practice the alphabet!
name:
©1998 by Evan-Moor Corp.

I use the computer to practice the alphabet!
name:
©1998 by Evan-Moor Corp.

I use the computer to practice the alphabet!
name:
©1998 by Evan-Moor Corp.

I use the computer to practice the alphabet!
name:
©1998 by Evan-Moor Corp.

Note: Use the cards on pages 12–15 to teach and practice terms and icons used on student direction pages.

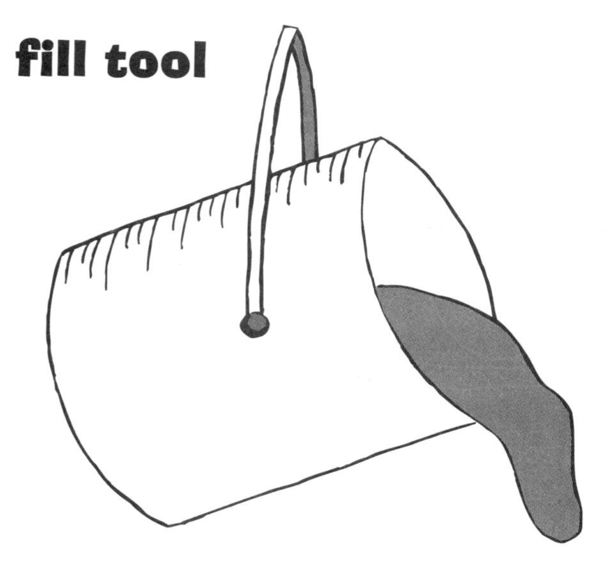

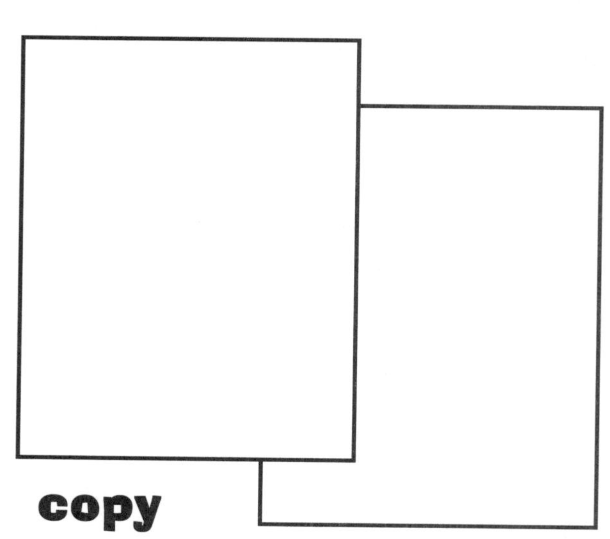

stamp

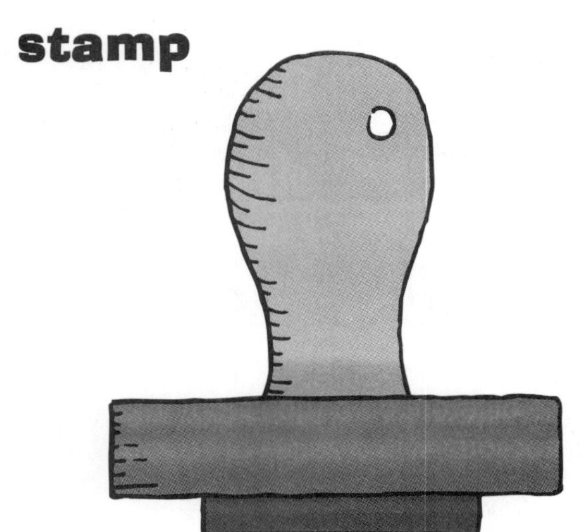

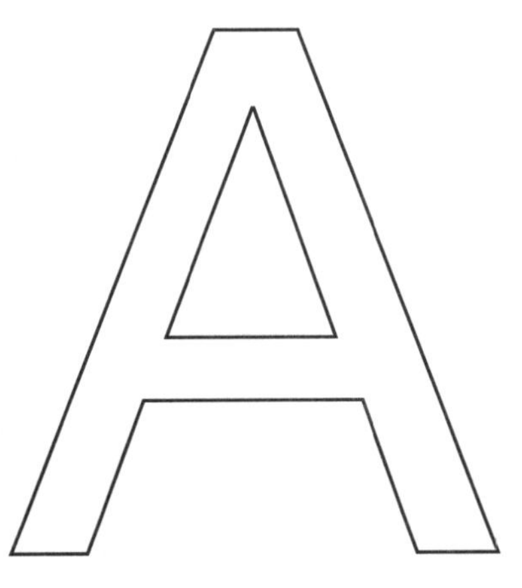

letter stamps

painting tool

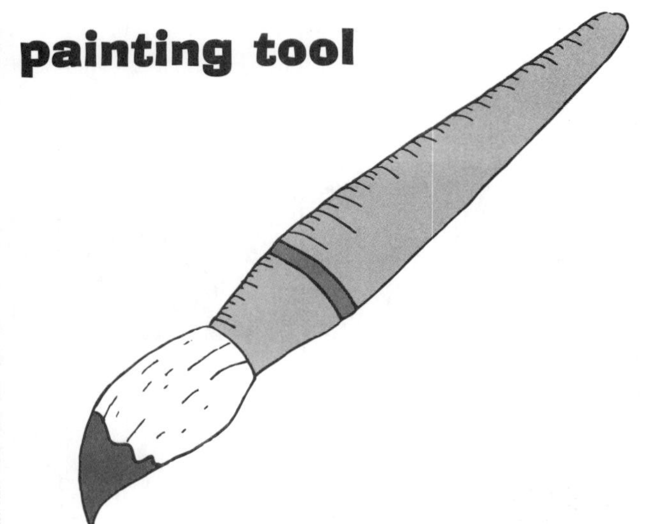

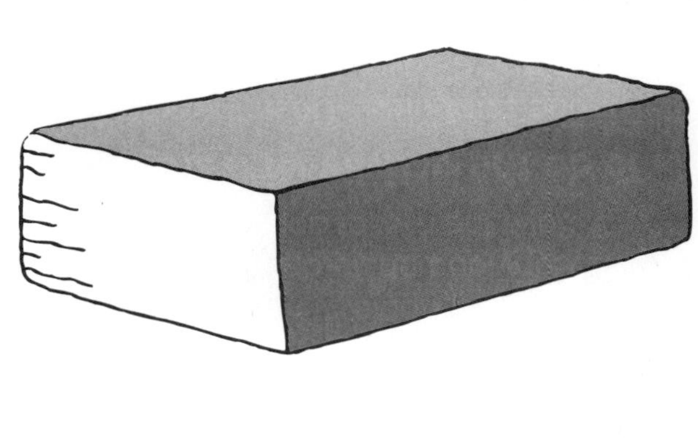

eraser

color

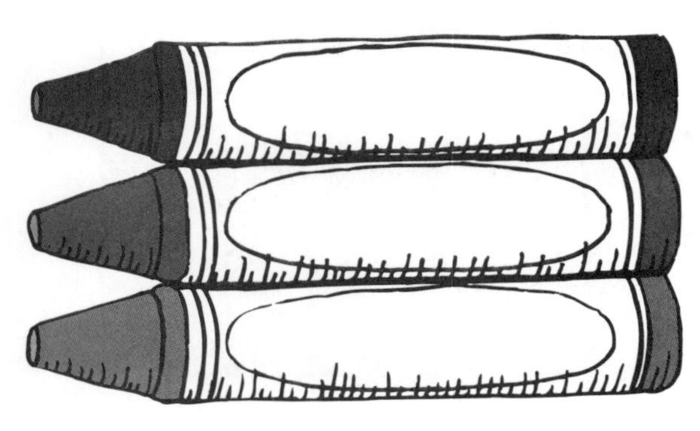

keyboard

print

choose

select

textured color

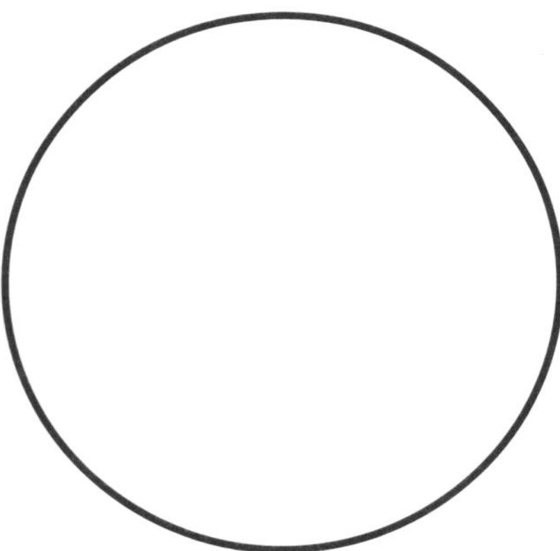

circle tool

square tool

add

pattern

designs

mouse

draw

line tool

Aa

A Row of Apples

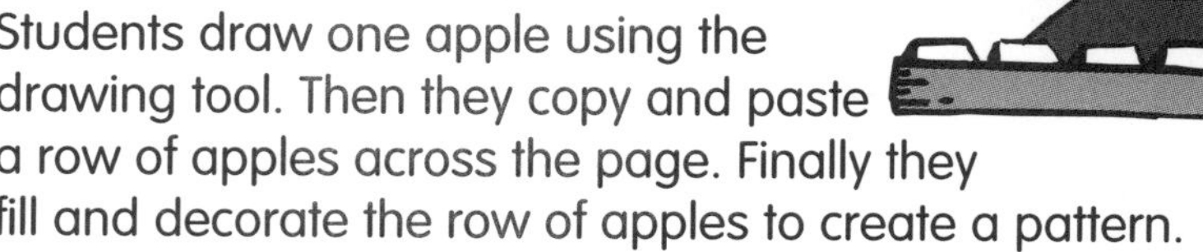

Students draw one apple using the drawing tool. Then they copy and paste a row of apples across the page. Finally they fill and decorate the row of apples to create a pattern.

Step by Step

1. Start with a clean screen.
2. Choose the drawing tool. Pick a line width.
3. Draw an apple.
4. Copy the apple.
5. Paste apples in a row.
6. Make a pattern with color.
7. Add a pattern with details.
   Suggest: leaves, worms, spots, and bites
8. Read your pattern.
9. Print the page.

Extending the Activity

- Challenge students to create several patterns on the single row of apples.
- Challenge students to label each pattern using the letter stamps.

Literature Connections

Alligator Arrived with Apples by Crescent Dragonwagon; Macmillan, 1987.
An Apple Tree Through the Year by Claudia Schnieper; Carolrhoda Books, Inc., 1987.
Applebet, an ABC by Clyde Watson; Farrar, Straus and Giroux, 1982.
Picking Apples and Pumpkins by Amy and Richard Hutchings; Scholastic Inc., 1994.
Ten Apples Up on Top by Theo LeSieg; Beginner Books, 1961.
The Year of Arnold's Apple Tree by Gail Gibbons; Harcourt Brace Jovanovich, 1984.

Note: Instruct students to choose a "fat"line as they are much easier to draw with than skinny lines.

A Row of Apples

1 Start with a clean screen.

2 Choose the drawing tool.
Pick a line width.

3 Draw an apple.

4 Copy the apple.

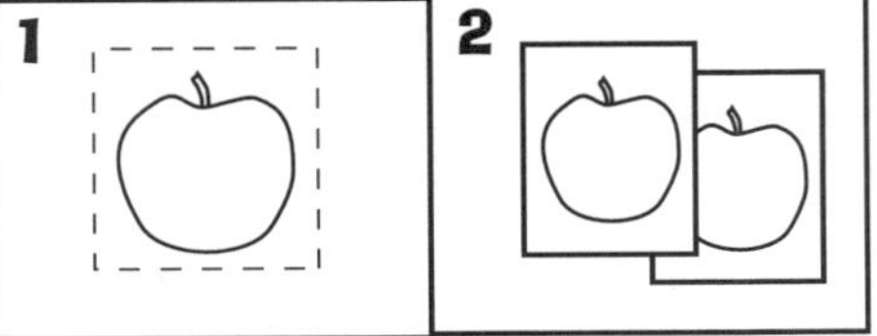

1 2

5 Paste apples in a row.

Paste

6 Make a pattern with color.

1 2

red green red green

7 Add a pattern with details.

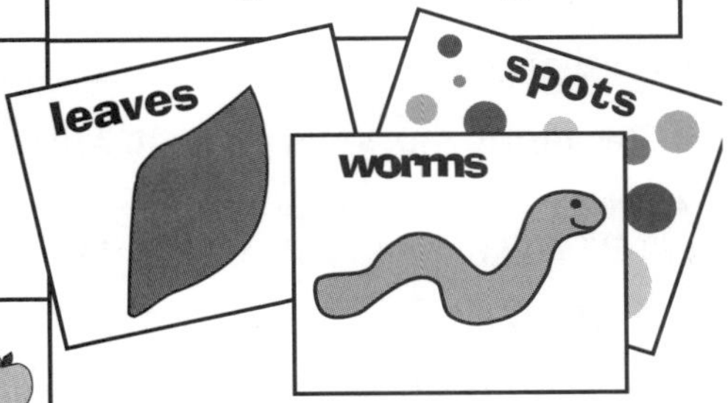

leaves spots worms

8 Read your pattern.

9 Print the page.

Bb

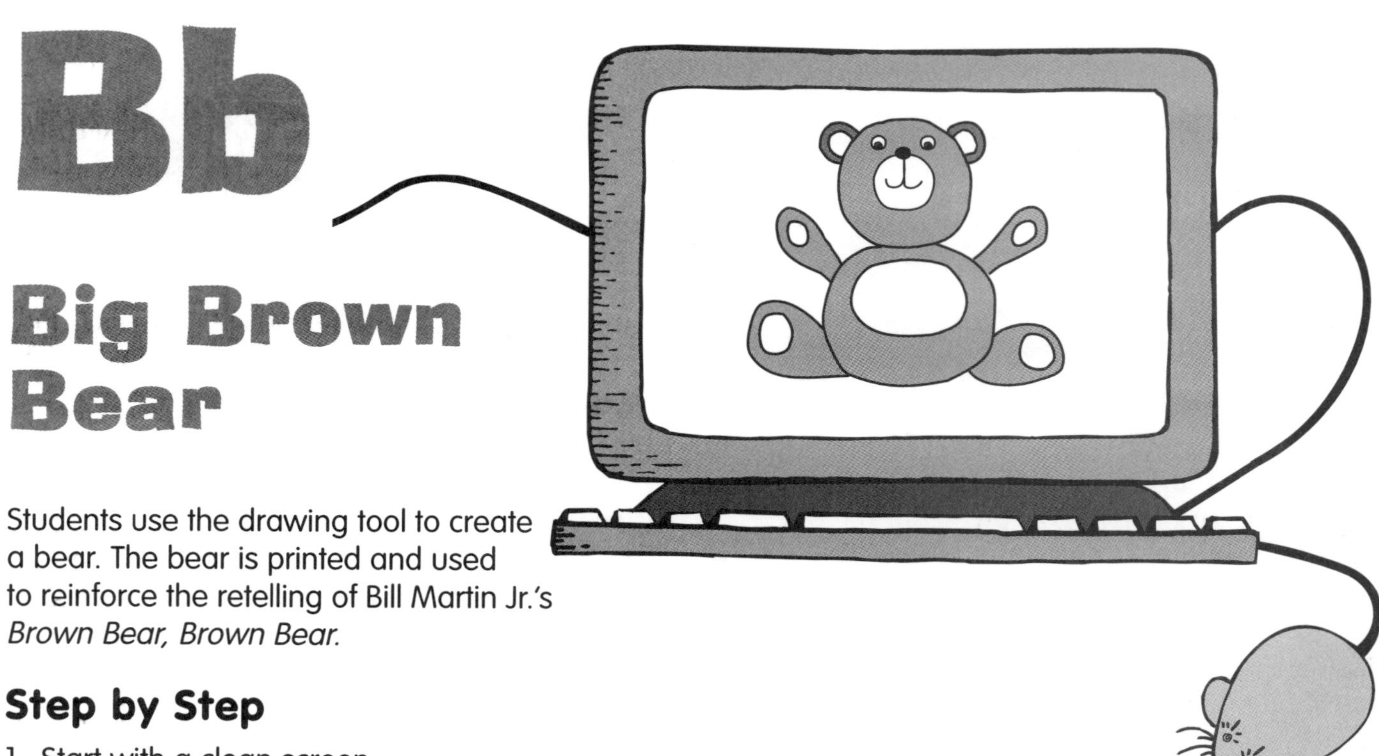

Big Brown Bear

Students use the drawing tool to create a bear. The bear is printed and used to reinforce the retelling of Bill Martin Jr.'s *Brown Bear, Brown Bear.*

Step by Step

1. Start with a clean screen.
2. Choose the drawing tool.
3. Pick a line width.
4. Pick the color.
5. Draw a bear.
6. Fill the bear with a color.
7. Print the page.

Extending the Activity

- Draw only bear faces and print them to use as masks to act out the question-answer story of *Brown Bear, Brown Bear.*
- Have students draw the brown bear on one side of the screen and another **b** thing on the other side of the screen. Type the words at the bottom of the page. Print the page. Fold in half and add a title on the outside cover. Have students read their "book."
- Print only the outlines of the bears and have students color them using markers or crayons.

Literature Connections

The Berenstain's B Book by Stanley and Janice Berenstain; Random House, 1971.
Bear by John Schoenherr; Philomel Books, 1991.
Bear Hugs by Kathleen Hague; Henry Holt and Company, 1989.
The Best Loved Bear by Diana Noonan; Ashton Scholastic, 1994.
Brown Bear, Brown Bear by Bill Martin Jr.; Holt, Rinehart, & Winston, 1983.
Sam's Teddy Bear by Barbro Lindgren; Morrow, 1982.

Big Brown Bear

1 Start with a clean screen.

2 Choose the drawing tool.

3 Pick a line width.

4 Pick the color.

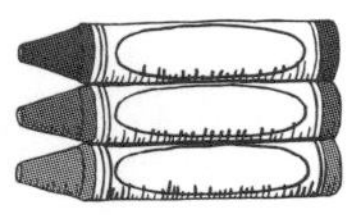

5 Draw a bear.

6 Fill the bear with a color.

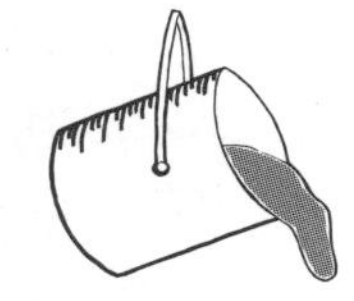

7 Print the page.

Catch a Colorful Caterpillar

Students draw a caterpillar by connecting **c**'s.

Step by Step

1. Start with a clean screen.
2. Choose the drawing tool. Pick a line width.
3. Choose a color.
4. Make the letter **c**.
5. Draw more **c**'s to make a caterpillar.
6. Add a head, antennae, and a face.
7. Fill with color.
8. Add designs.
9. Print the page.

Extending the Activity

- Use the stamp tool to stamp a picture of something that begins with the letter **c** in each section of the caterpillar.
- Fill the sections of the caterpillar to create a pattern.
- Have each student create one section of a caterpillar using a template. (See page 4 for directions for making a template.) Print the decorated sections and cut them out. Connect the sections to make a colorful class caterpillar.

Literature Connections

The Caterpillar and the Polliwog by Jack Kent; Prentice-Hall, 1982.
Caterpillar to Butterfly by Oliver S. Owen; Abdo & Daughters, 1994.
Sometimes Things Change by Patricia Eastman; Children's Press, 1983.
The Very Hungry Caterpillar by Eric Carle; Collins Publishers, 1979.

Catch a Colorful Caterpillar

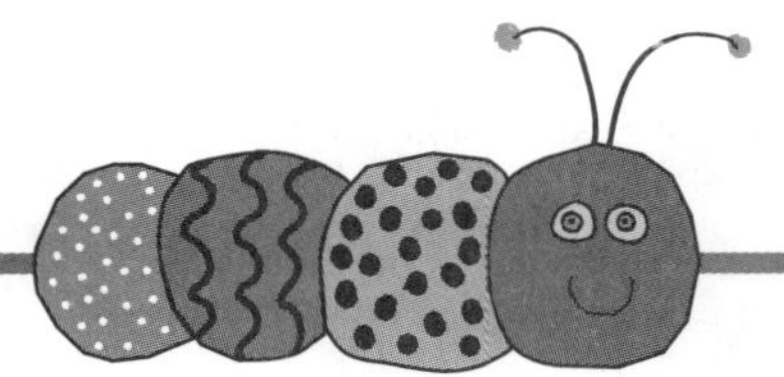

1 Start with a clean screen.

2 Choose the drawing tool. Pick a line width.

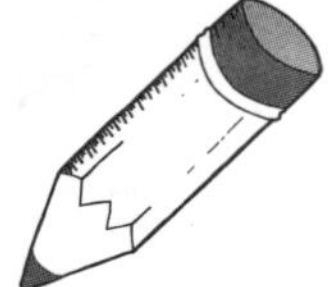

3 Choose a color.

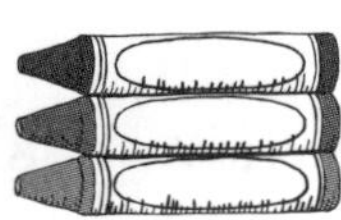

4 Make the letter **c**.

5 Draw more **c**'s to make a caterpillar.

6 Add a head, antennae, and a face.

7 Fill with color.

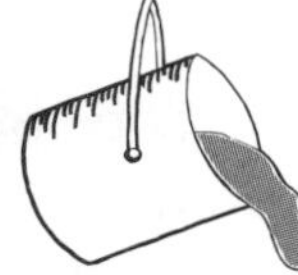

8 Add designs.

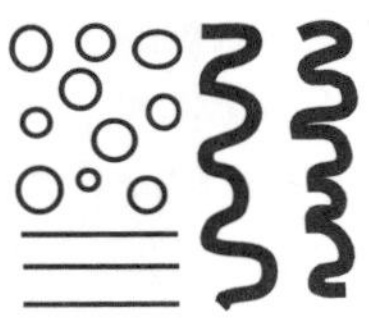

9 Print the page.

Delightful Dinosaurs

Students create dinosaurs using the drawing and painting tools.

Step by Step

1. Start with a clean screen.
2. Choose the drawing tool, a color, and a line width.
3. Draw a dinosaur.
4. Pick the fill tool. Color your dinosaur.
5. Choose the drawing tool, a color, and a line width.
6. Draw a home for your dinosaur.
7. Print the page.

Extending the Activity

- Read *A Dinosaur Like Me* by Bernard Most, and have students create and name dinosaurs that are like themselves as modeled in the book.
- Encourage students to tell about their dinosaur. Type their words at the bottom of the picture. Use the pages to create a class dinosaur book.
- Organize the dinosaurs by size after they are printed. Make a display called *Big Dinosaurs and Small Dinosaurs.*

Literature Connections

Dad's Dinosaur Day by Diane Dawson Hearn; Macmillan, 1993.
Dinosaur by Gail Gibbons; Holiday House, 1987.
Dinosaurs by Michael Emberly; Little, Brown and Company, 1980.
Dinosaur Garden by Liza Donnelly; Scholastic, 1990.
The Dinosaur Who Lived in My Backyard by Barbara Hennessy; Viking Kestrel, 1988.
What Happened to Patrick's Dinosaurs? by Carol Carrick; Clarion Books, 1986.

Delightful Dinosaurs

1 Start with a clean screen.

2 Choose the drawing tool, a color, and a line width.

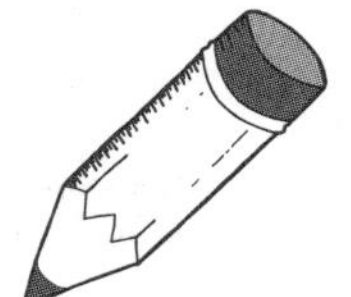

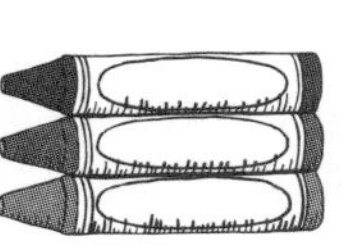

3 Draw a dinosaur.

4 Pick the fill tool.
Color your dinosaur.

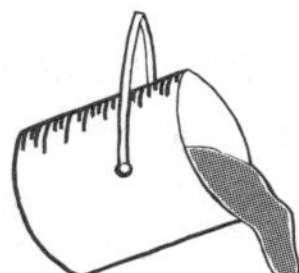

5 Choose the drawing tool, a color, and a line width.

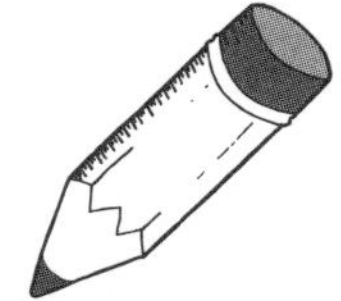

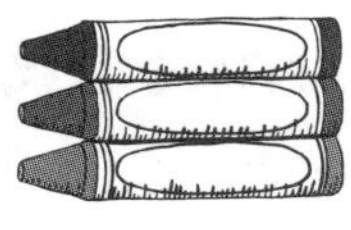

6 Draw a home for your dinosaur.

7 Print the page.

Easy Eggs

Students decorate eggs using the drawing tool and the fill tool.

Step by Step

1. Start with a clean screen.
2. Choose the circle tool. Pick a color.
3. Make an egg.
4. Choose the drawing tool. Choose a line width.
5. Pick a color.
6. Add dots and lines.
7. Print the page.

For a pretty egg tree:

- Cut the eggs out and mount them on poster board.
- Add ribbon loops for hanging.
- Hang eggs on the branch.

Extending the Activity

- Students copy the outline of the egg onto a second page and draw the animal or bird that will hatch from the egg inside the outline. Print the two pages, cut out the eggs, and fasten them together to create flip-open eggs.
- Create a display of oviparous creatures and their eggs after reading *Chickens Aren't the Only Ones. (See book list below.)* Students love using such a big word!

Literature Connections

Chickens Aren't the Only Ones by Ruth Heller; Grosset and Dunlap, 1981.
Egg by Robert Burton; Dorling Kindersley, 1994.
Egg! by A. J. Wood; Little, Brown and Company, 1993.
Hatch, Egg, Hatch by Shen Roddie and Frances Cony; Little, Brown and Company, 1991.
The Most Wonderful Egg by Helme Heine; Atheneum, 1983.
Too Many Eggs by M. Christina Butler; David R. Godine, 1988.
Zinnia and Dot by Lisa Campbell Ernst; Viking, 1992.

Easy Eggs

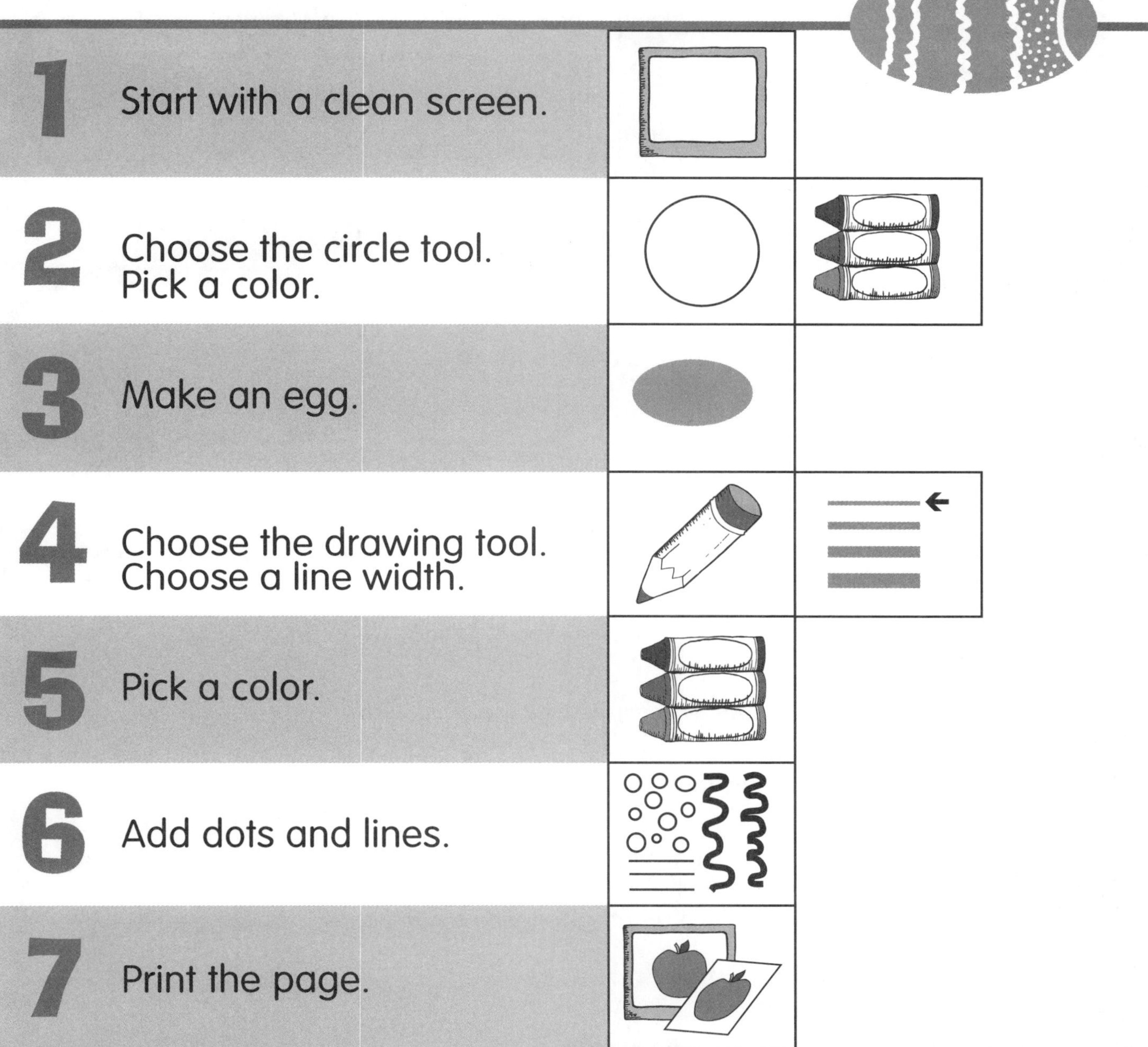

1 Start with a clean screen.

2 Choose the circle tool.
Pick a color.

3 Make an egg.

4 Choose the drawing tool.
Choose a line width.

5 Pick a color.

6 Add dots and lines.

7 Print the page.

Fancy Fish

Students draw and decorate fish using the drawing and fill tools.

Step by Step

1. Start with a clean screen.
2. Choose the drawing tool, a color, and a line width.
3. Draw the water.
4. Pick the fill tool. Make the water blue.
5. Draw a fish.
6. Pick the fill tool.
7. Use many pretty colors to fill in your picture.
8. Print the page.

Extending the Activity

- Have students use geometric shapes to decorate their fish. Then, have them count the number of shapes used on each fish.
- Draw a large blue circle and use the fancy fish to create math problems in the style of *Splash.* (See book list below.)
- Save the fish picture. Copy the fish and paste it to make a two-fish picture. Save the second picture. Repeat copying the single fish, pasting it onto the newest page to make a three-fish picture, and then saving. Use the saved pictures in a counting fish slide show (page 6) or print them to make a counting book.

Literature Connections

Big Al by Andrew Clements; Picture Book Studio, 1988.
Blue Sea by Robert Kalan; Greenwillow Books, 1979.
Fish Eyes by Lois Ehlert; Harcourt Brace, 1990.
Ocean Parade: a Counting Book by Patricia MacCarthy; Dial Books for Young Readers, 1990.
The Rainbow Fish by Marcus Pfister; North-South Books, 1992.
Splash by Ann Jonas; Greenwillow Books, 1995.
Swimmy by Leo Lionni; Knopf, 1963.

Fancy Fish

1 Start with a clean screen.

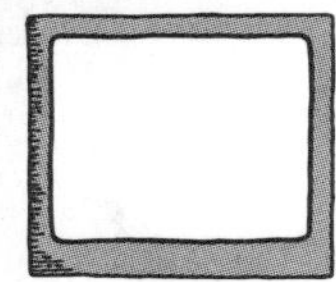

2 Choose the drawing tool, a color, and a line width.

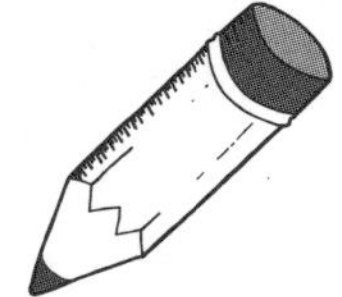
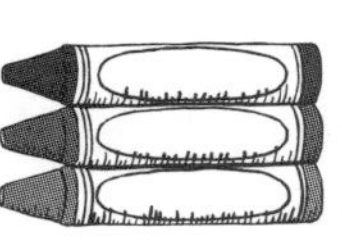

3 Draw the water.

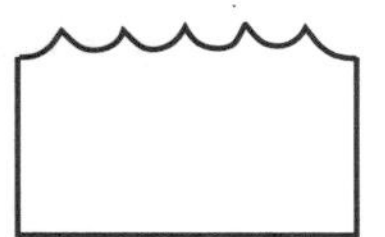

4 Pick the fill tool. Make the water blue.

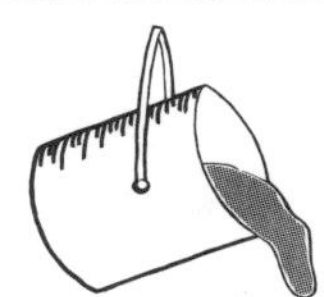
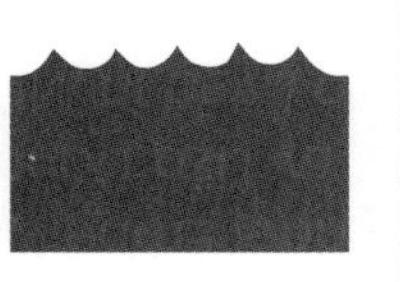

5 Draw the fish.

1 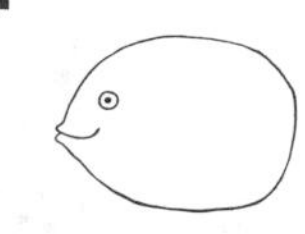
2 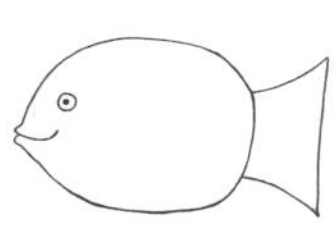
3 

6 Pick the fill tool.

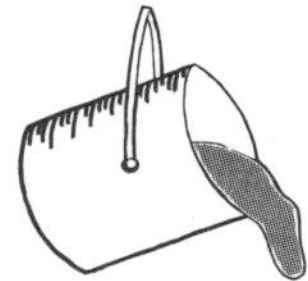

7 Use many pretty colors to fill in your picture.

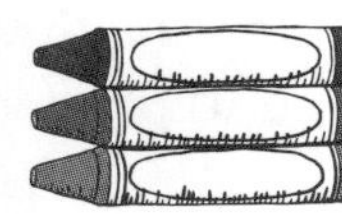

8 Print the page.

Gg

A Gaggle of Geese

Students create geese by erasing background color to create the white goose.

Step by Step

1. Start with a clean screen.
2. Fill the screen with color.
3. Choose a small erasing tool.
4. Erase a goose shape.
5. Choose the drawing tool.
6. Pick a line width.
7. Choose a color.
8. Add a beak, eyes, wing, and feet.
9. Print the page.

Extending the Activity

- Talk about the special **g** names given to different geese -- goose, gander, and gosling. Have students draw a family of geese, labeling them to show that they understand the differences. (goose = mother, gander = father, and gosling = child)
- Copy and paste the goose to create a page that shows the singular and plural forms. Do the same for other animals starting with the **g** sound (gorilla, garter snake, gecko, goldfish, grizzly bear). Bind the singular/plural pages into a class book entitled *One and More Than One*.

Literature Connections

The Day the Goose Got Loose by Reeve Lindbergh; Scholastic Inc., 1990.
Goose by Molly Bang; The Blue Sky Press, 1996.
Petunia by Roger Duvoisin; Knopf, 1987.

A Gaggle of Geese

1 Start with a clean screen.

2 Fill the screen with color.

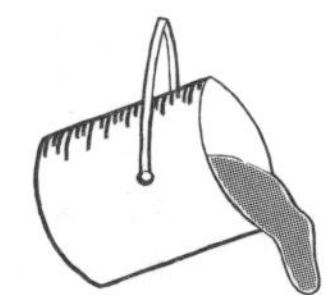

3 Choose a small erasing tool.

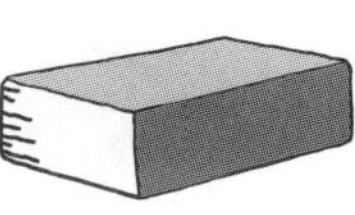

4 Erase a goose shape.

5 Choose the drawing tool.

6 Pick a line width.

7 Choose a color.

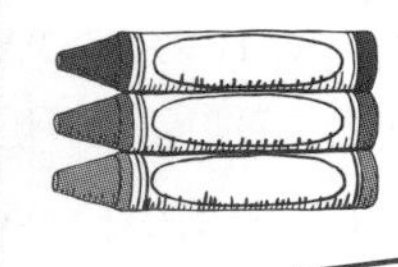

8 Add a beak, eyes, wing, and feet.

9 Print the page.

Hh

Hats, Hats, Hats

Students draw hats using the drawing and painting tools. Then they label the hats with a short description and print the pages to create a class book.

Step by Step

1. Start with a clean screen.
2. Choose the drawing tool.
3. Pick a line width.
4. Choose a color.
5. Draw a hat.
6. Add colors and designs.
7. Choose the keyboard.
8. Tell about your hat.
9. Print the page.

To make a class book:

- Print full size.
- Add a first page and an identical last page that says, "Hats, hats, hats."
- Bind the pages and enjoy the book.

Extending the Activity

Have a Hat Day. Encourage students to wear a hat to school. Use your computer camera to take pictures of each student. Copy the pictures into a computer slide show. (See page 6.) Record students' oral descriptions of their hats to narrate the slide show.

Literature Connections

Caps for Sale by Esphyr Slobodkina; W. R. Scott, 1947.
A Hat for Minerva Louise by Janet Morgan Stoeke; Dutton Children's Books, 1994.
The Hat by Jan Brett; G. P. Putnam's Sons, 1997.
Martin's Hats by Joan W. Blos; Morrow, 1984.
Old Hat, New Hat by Stan and Jan Berenstain; Random House, 1970.

Hats, Hats, Hats

1 Start with a clean screen.

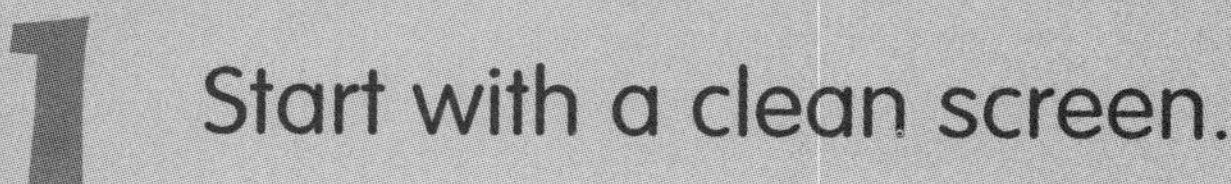

2 Choose the drawing tool.

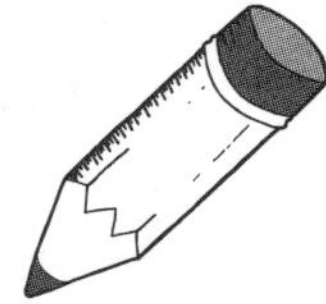

3 Pick a line width.

4 Choose a color.

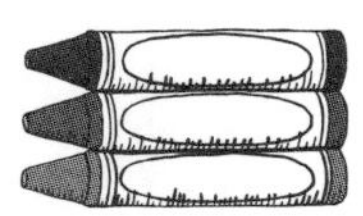

5 Draw a hat.

6 Add colors and designs.

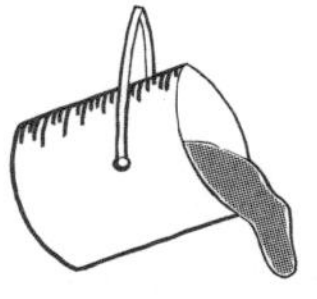

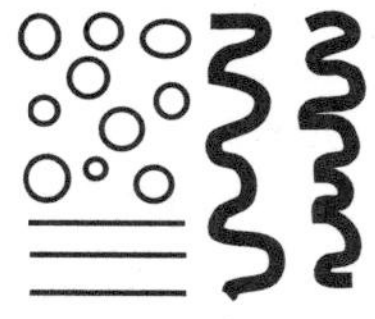

7 Choose the keyboard.

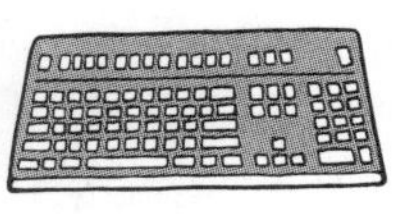

8 Tell about your hat.

My purple hat has stars on it.

9 Print the page.

Ii

Incredible Insects

Students use the circle and line tools to create an insect.

Step by Step

1. Start with a clean screen.
2. Choose the circle tool and a color.
3. Make 3 circles on the screen.
4. Choose the line tool, a color, and a line width.
5. Add 6 legs and 2 antennae.
6. Choose the drawing tool, a color, and a thin line width.
7. Add eyes, wings, spots, stripes, and feet.
8. Print the page.

Extending the Activity

Make a list of the incredible insects that live in your environment. Use the insect illustrations that your students have created to decorate the list.

Literature Connections

The Best Bug Parade by Stuart J. Murphy; Harper Collins Publishers, 1996.
Bugs by Nancy Winslow Parker and Joan Richards Wright; Greenwillow Books, 1987.
Fireflies! by Julie Brinckloe; Collier Macmillan, 1985.
How Many Bugs in a Box? by David A. Carter; Little Simon, 1988.
One Hundred Hungry Ants by Elinor J. Pinczes; Houghton Mifflin Company, 1993.

Incredible Insects

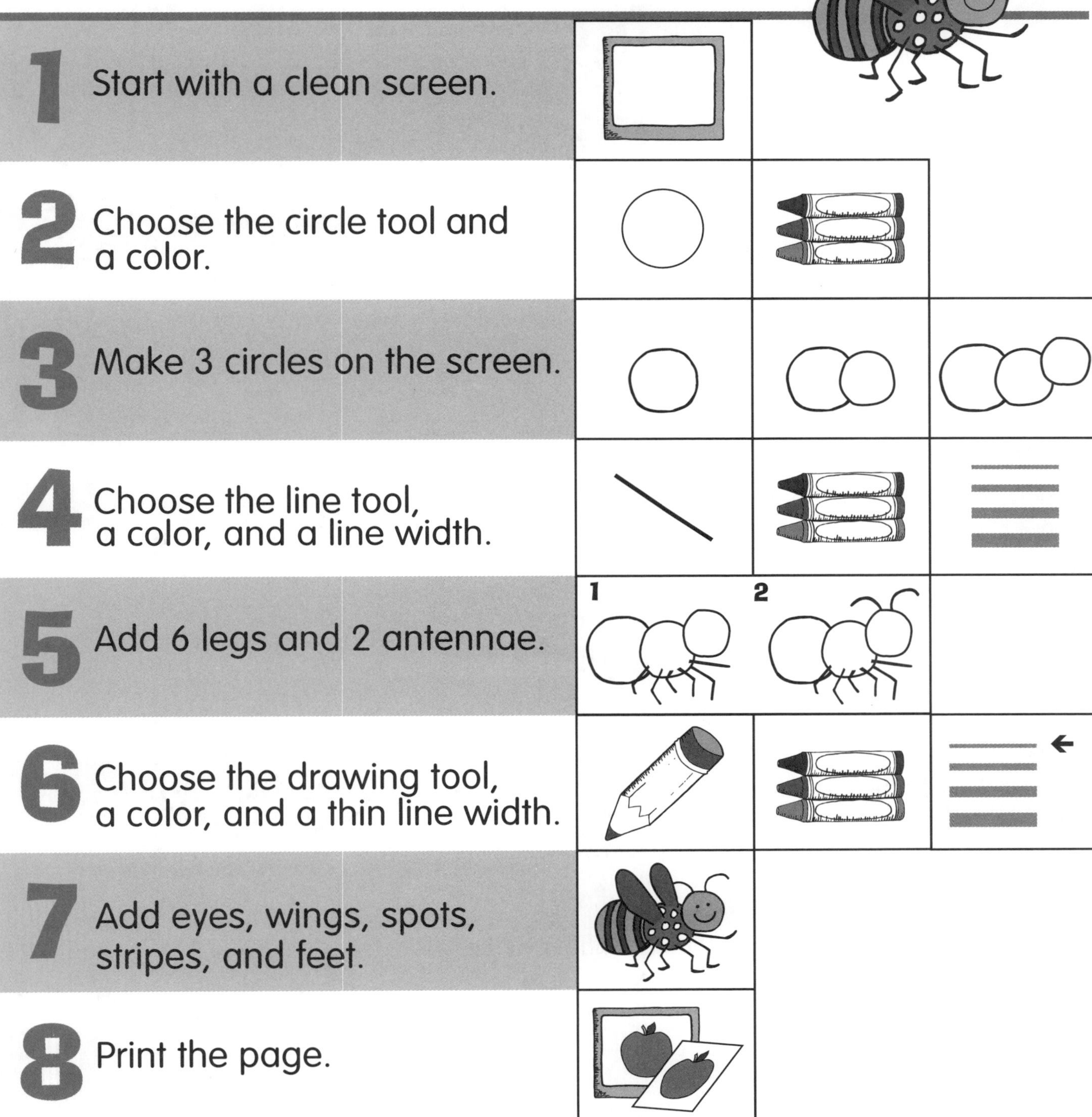

1 Start with a clean screen.

2 Choose the circle tool and a color.

3 Make 3 circles on the screen.

4 Choose the line tool, a color, and a line width.

5 Add 6 legs and 2 antennae.

6 Choose the drawing tool, a color, and a thin line width.

7 Add eyes, wings, spots, stripes, and feet.

8 Print the page.

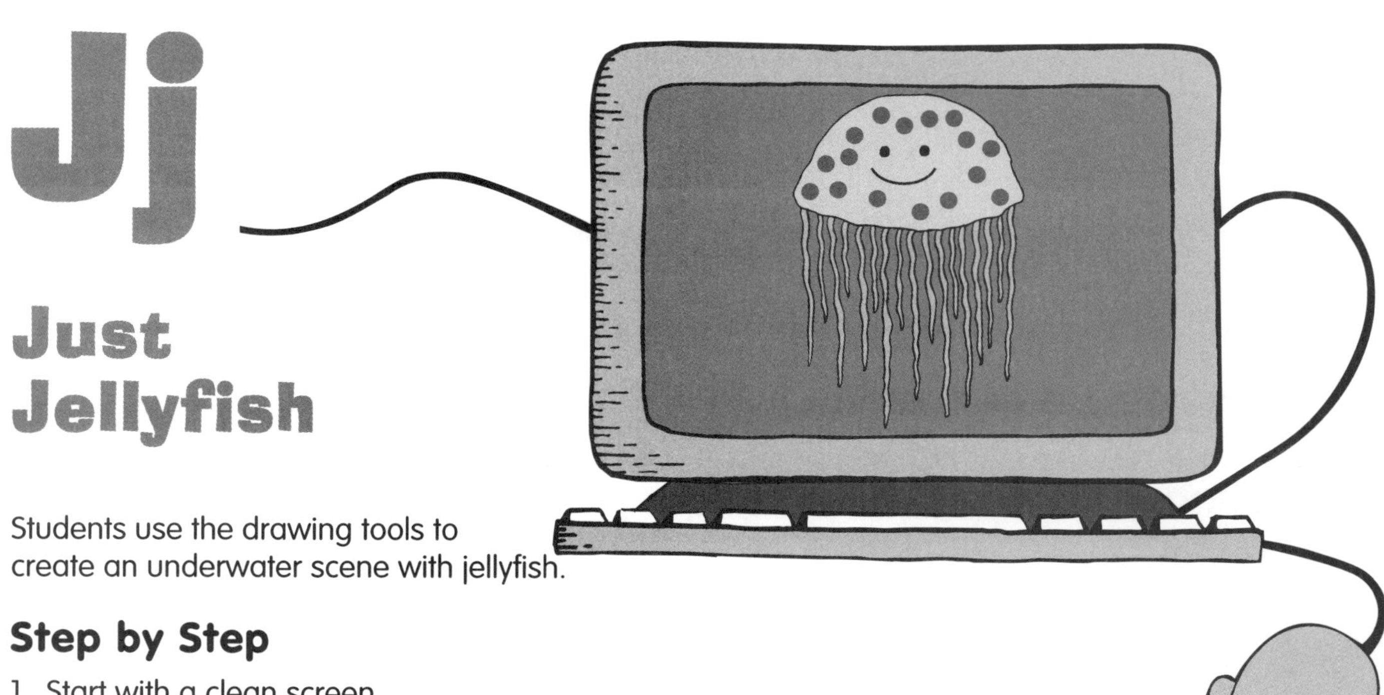

Jj

Just Jellyfish

Students use the drawing tools to create an underwater scene with jellyfish.

Step by Step

1. Start with a clean screen.
2. Choose the fill tool and the color blue.
3. Color the screen blue.
4. Choose the drawing tool, a color, and a medium line width.
5. Draw the jellyfish.
6. Choose the fill tool and a color.
7. Color the jellyfish.
8. Choose the drawing tool, a color, and a narrow line width.
9. Add details.

Extending the Activity

Print out the jellyfish pictures. Use the pictures as a background for a diorama by pasting them on the bottom of a shallow box. Stand the box on its side. Add kelp cutouts. Make a jellyfish cutout and mount it on the kelp to add dimension.

Literature Connections

The Ocean Alphabet Book by Jerry Pallotta; Charlesbridge, 1986.
Sea Shapes by Suse MacDonald; Gulliver Books, 1994.

Just Jellyfish

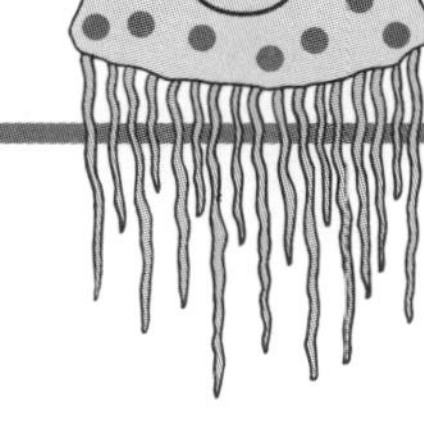

1 Start with a clean screen.			
2 Choose the fill tool and the color blue.	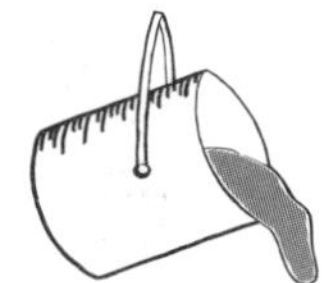	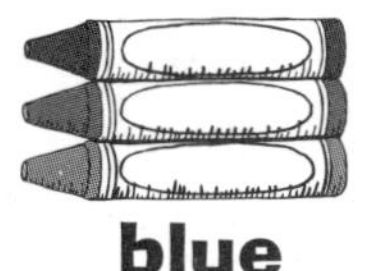 blue	
3 Color the screen blue.			
4 Choose the drawing tool, a color, and a medium line.		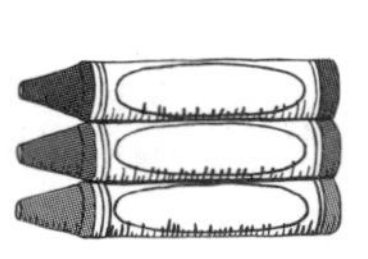	
5 Draw the jellyfish.	1 	2  	3 
6 Choose the fill tool and a color.	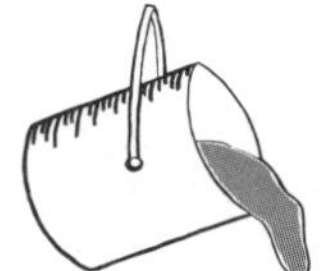	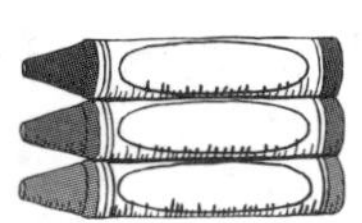	
7 Color the jellyfish.			
8 Choose the drawing tool, a color, and a narrow line.	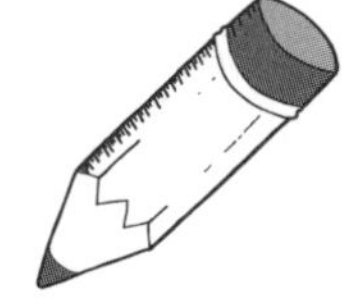	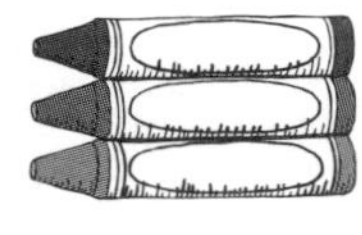	
9 Add details.	spots 	stripes 	

Kites

Students draw a kite using the drawing tools and write a sentence about the kite.

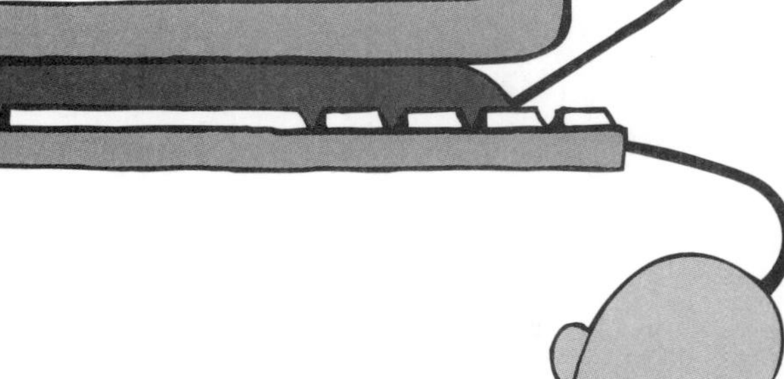

Step by Step

1. Start with a clean screen.
2. Choose the drawing tool, a line width, and a color.
3. Draw a kite.
4. Divide the kite into 4 parts.
5. Choose the fill tool. Pick a color.
6. Color the kite.
7. Choose keyboard or letter stamps.
8. Write about the kite.
9. Print the page.

Extending the Activity

- Have students dictate a story about their kite.

  If I were a kite I would...

  My kite flew away. I think it...

- Using the smallest mode, print the kites, and trim paper to desired size. Add numerals to one corner and use them as calendar markers for a windy month.

Literature Connections

The Emperor and the Kite by Jane Yolen; Philomel Books, 1988.
Kite Flier by David Wiesner; Collier Macmillan, 1986.
Kite Flying is for Me by Tom Moran; Lerner Publications Inc., 1984.

Kites

1 Start with a clean screen.

2 Choose the drawing tool, a line width, and a color.

3 Draw a kite.

4 Divide the kite into 4 parts.

5 Choose the fill tool. Pick a color.

6 Color the kite.

7 Choose keyboard or letter stamps.

8 Write about the kite.

My kite ...

9 Print the page.

Lovely Lavender Lines

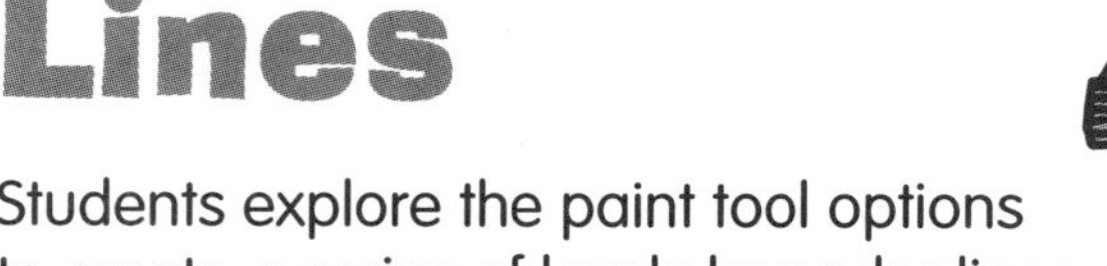

Students explore the paint tool options to create a series of lovely lavender lines.

Step by Step

1. Start with a clean screen.
2. Choose the paint tool.
3. Pick lavender.
4. Draw many different kinds of lines.
5. Print the page.

Extending the Activity

- Have students use letter stamps or the keyboard to place their names in the center of the screen and then decorate them by drawing around their names with different lines. Post the printed names in a long class list.
- Have students make little lines and long lines to create patterns. Label the lines.

Literature Connections

Harold and the Purple Crayon by Crockett Johnson; Harper & Row, 1955.
Lily's Purple Plastic Purse by Kevin Henkes; Greenwillow Books, 1996.

Lovely Lavender Lines

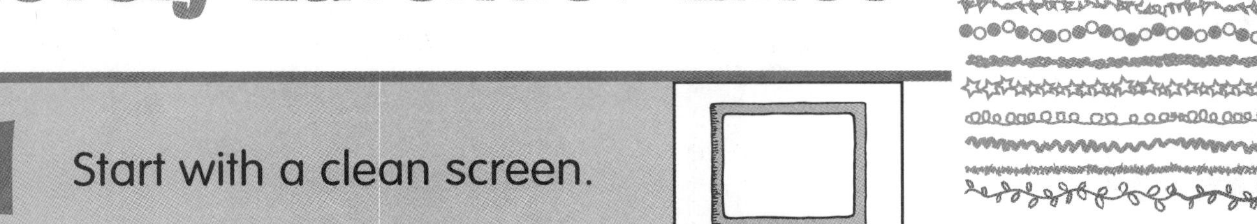

1 Start with a clean screen.

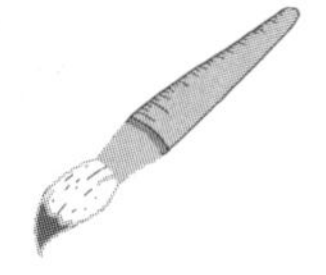

2 Choose the paint tool.

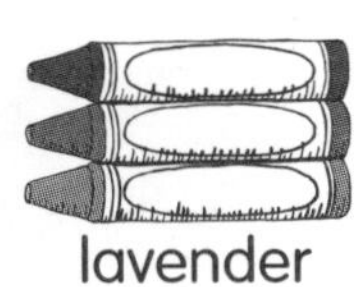

3 Pick lavender.

lavender

4 Draw many different kinds of lines.

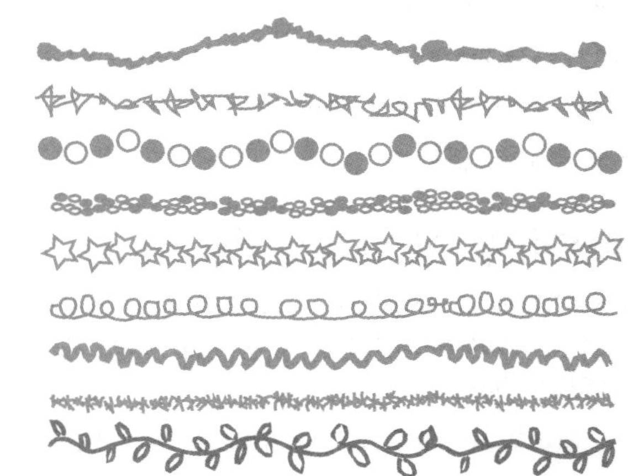

5 Print the page.

Mm

Musical Mice

Students create mice with musical instruments. Then they use the circle and the line tools to create music notes.

Step by Step

1. Start with a clean screen.
2. Choose the drawing tool, a line width, and a color.
3. Draw a mouse.
4. Draw an instrument for the mouse.
5. Choose the fill tool.
6. Color the mouse.
7. Choose the circle tool. Make little circles.
8. Choose the line tool. Add lines to the little circles.
9. Print the page.

Extending the Lesson

- Imagine what the mouse music would sound like. Choose students to become the mice and act out a mouse concert.
- Lead the students in singing a mouse song.

"Three Blind Mice, Three Blind Mice..."

Literature Connections

Come Out and Play, Little Mouse by Robert Kraus; Greenwillow Books, 1987.
Frederick by Leo Lionni; Random House, 1973.
Mouse Count and *Mouse Paint* by Ellen Stoll Walsh; Harcourt Brace & Co., 1991.
The Pea Patch Jig by Thatcher Hurd; Crown, 1986.
Picnic by Emily Arnold McCully; Harper and Row, 1984.

Musical Mice

1 Start with a clean screen.

2 Choose the drawing tool, a line width, and a color.

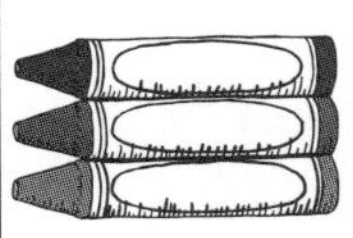

3 Draw a mouse.

4 Draw an instrument for the mouse.

5 Choose the fill tool.

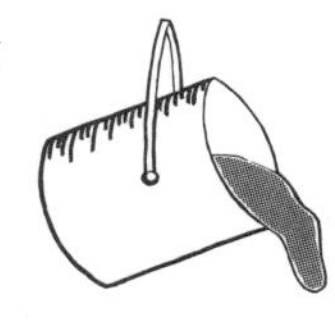

6 Color the mouse.

7 Choose the circle tool. Make little circles.

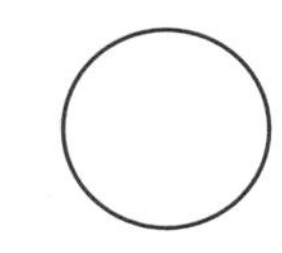
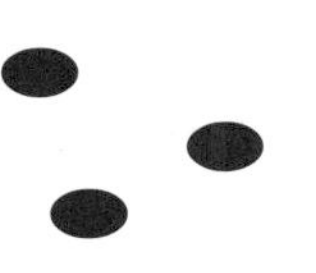

8 Choose the line tool. Add lines to the little circles.

9 Print the page.

Nn

Nifty Nests

Students create a nifty nest with the line tool.

Step by Step

1. Start with a clean screen.
2. Choose the line tool.
3. Pick a color.
4. Choose a line width.
5. Make a nest using the lines.
6. Add more lines of different colors and different sizes.
7. Draw a bird in the nest.
8. Print the page.

Extending the Activity

- Use the dialogue balloon in the paint brush options to create a dialogue balloon for the bird. Have students dictate or type something that the bird might be saying as it sits in the nest.

  I really want a new nest.

  This is the best nest.

  I'm hungry. I think I'll look for a worm.

- Have students describe their nests. Keyboard their descriptions. Create a realtor's ad book for birds in the market for a new nest.

  Looking for a new nest? Check out the *New Nest News*!

Literature Connections

The Best Nest by P. D. Eastman; Beginner Books, 1968.
Birds' Nests by Eileen Curran; Troll Associates, 1985.
Feathers for Lunch by Lois Ehlert; Harcourt Brace, 1990.
The Magpies' Nest by Joanna Foster; Clarion Books, 1995.

Nifty Nests

1 Start with a clean screen.

2 Choose the line tool.

3 Pick a color.

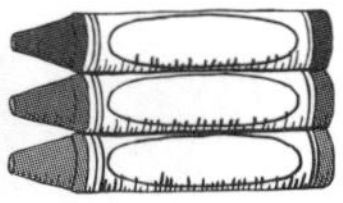

4 Choose a line width.

5 Make a nest using the lines.

6 Add more lines of different colors and different sizes.

7 Draw a bird in the nest.

8 Print the page.

Oo

No Ordinary Octopus

Students will design and draw an octopus using the drawing and fill tools.

Step by Step

1. Start with a clean screen.
2. Choose the drawing tool and a line width.
3. Pick a color.
4. Draw an octopus.
5. Choose the fill tool.
6. Color the octopus.
7. Add a face, hair, and a necklace or a necktie.
8. Print the page.

Extending the Activity

- Have students give their octopuses names that begin with an **o** sound. Keyboard the name beneath the picture.
- Draw or stamp objects that begin with **o** in each of the octopus's "hands."

Literature Connections

How to Hide an Octopus and Other Sea Creatures by Ruth Heller; Grosset & Dunlap, 1985.
I Was All Thumbs by Bernard Waber; Houghton Mifflin, 1975.
Octopus Hug by Laurence Pringle; Boyd Mills Press, 1993.
An Octopus Is Amazing by Patricia Lauber; Crowell, 1990.
Otto Is Different by Franz Brandenberg; Greenwillow Books, 1985.

No Ordinary Octopus

1	Start with a clean screen.	
2	Choose the drawing tool and a line width.	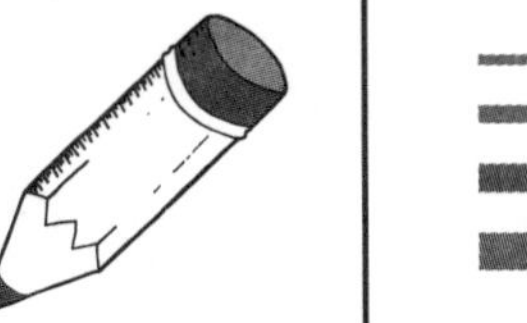 
3	Pick a color.	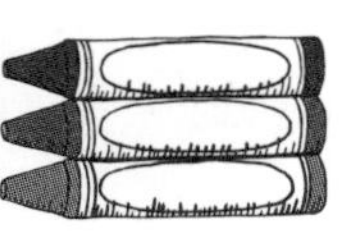
4	Draw an octopus.	 
5	Choose the fill tool.	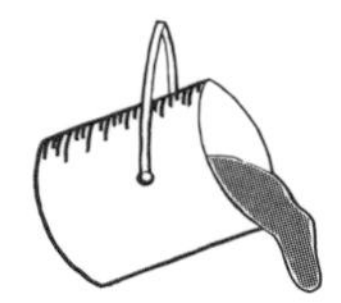
6	Color the octopus.	
7	Add a face, hair, and a necklace or a necktie.	
8	Print the page.	

Pp

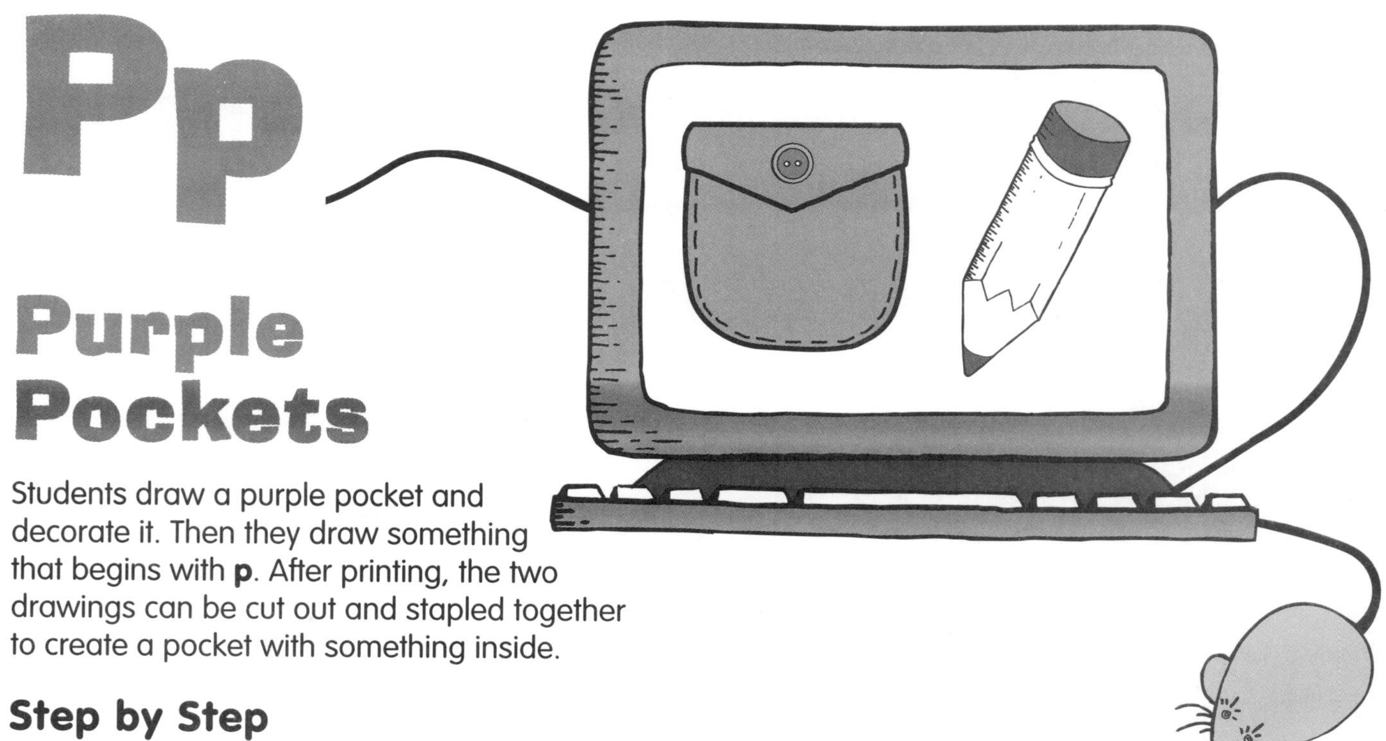

Purple Pockets

Students draw a purple pocket and decorate it. Then they draw something that begins with **p**. After printing, the two drawings can be cut out and stapled together to create a pocket with something inside.

Step by Step

1. Start with a clean screen.
2. Choose the drawing tool, a line width, and purple.
3. Draw a pocket on one side of your screen.
4. Choose the fill tool and the color purple.
5. Color the pocket.
6. Choose the drawing tool.
7. Add a button, stitching, a flap, and your name.
8. Draw something that begins with **p** beside the pocket.
9. Print the page.

Extending the Activity

- Have students copy and paste pockets across the screen. Then decorate and fill to create pocket patterns.
- Post the purple pockets on a bulletin board. Have students dictate descriptions of what's inside their pockets. Keyboard the descriptions and post with the pockets.

Literature Connections

Peter's Pockets by Judi Barrett; Atheneum, 1974.
A Pocket for Corduroy by Don Freeman; Viking Press, 1978.
What Have I Got? by Leonard Kessler; Harper, 1961.

Purple Pockets

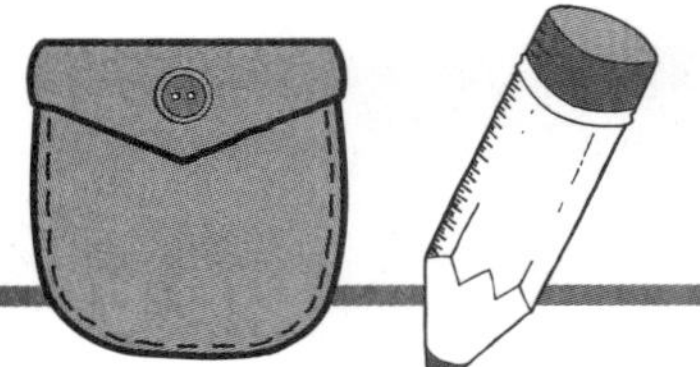

1 Start with a clean screen.			
2 Choose the drawing tool, a line width, and purple.	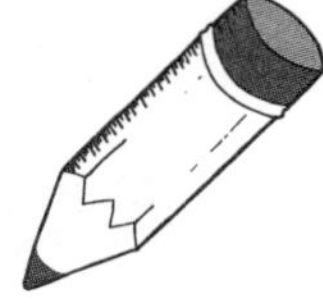	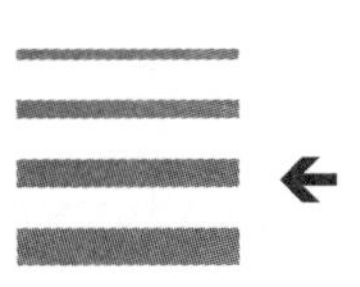	
3 Draw a pocket on one side of your screen.	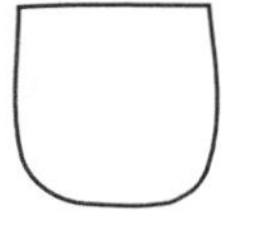		
4 Choose the fill tool and the color purple.	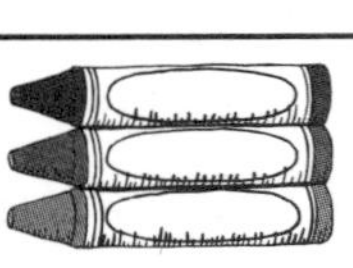		
5 Color the pocket.			
6 Choose the drawing tool.	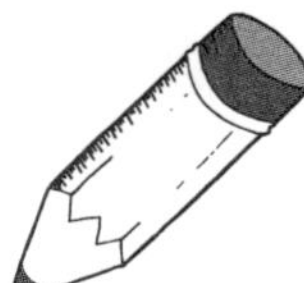		
7 Add a button, stitching, a flap, and your name.	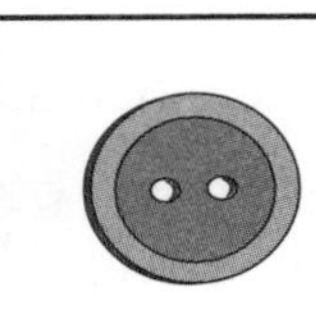	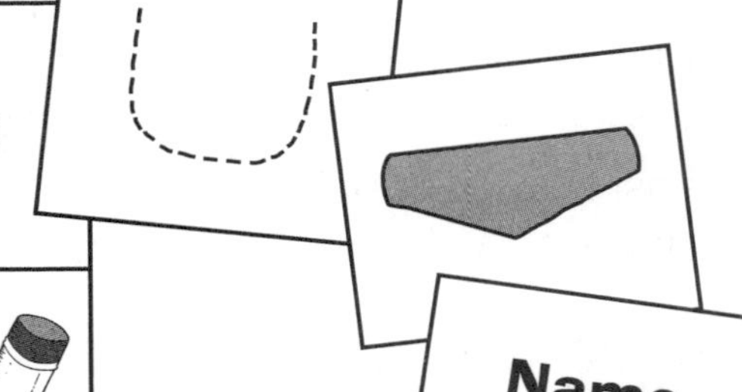	
8 Draw something that begins with **p** beside the pocket.			
9 Print the page.			

Qq

Quack, Quack, Quiet

Students draw a duck with the drawing tools. They add a speech bubble that says "Quack!" or "Quiet!"

Step by Step

1. Start with a clean screen.
2. Choose the drawing tool, a color, and a medium line.
3. Draw a duck.
4. Choose the fill tool.
5. Color your drawing.
6. Draw a speech bubble.
7. Keyboard "Quack!" or "Quiet!" into the bubble.
8. Read the screen.

Extending the Activity

- Print the pages and create a class book. Place several "Quack!" pages together and then follow with a "Quiet!" page. Students will love reading the pages.
- Think of quiet things. Have students draw quiet pictures. Then think of loud things and draw loud pictures. Keyboard a dictated sentence about the contrast.

Sleeping is quiet, but playing outside is loud.

Literature Connections

Duncan the Dancing Duck by Syd Hoff; Clarion Books, 1994.
Farmyard Sounds by Colin & Jacqui Hawkins; Crown, 1986.
Have You Seen My Duckling? by Nancy Tafuri; Greenwillow Books, 1984.
One Duck, Another Duck by Charlotte Pomerantz; Greenwillow Books, 1984.
Quacky Quack-Quack! by Ian Whybrow; Four Winds Press, 1991.
The Surprise Family by Lynn Reiser; Greenwillow Books, 1994.

Quack, Quack, Quiet

1 Start with a clean screen.

2 Choose the drawing tool, a color, and a medium line.

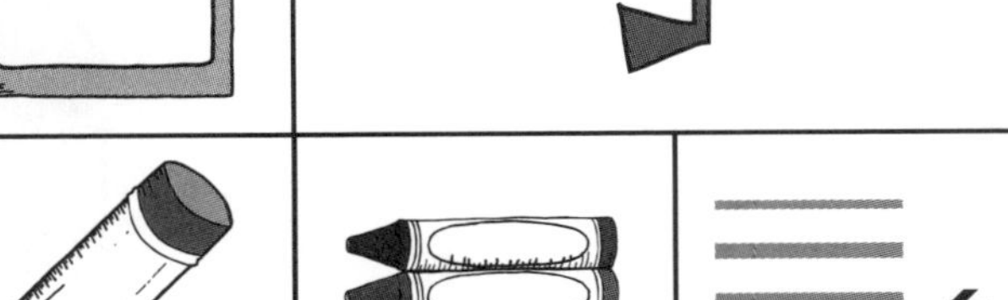

3 Draw a duck.

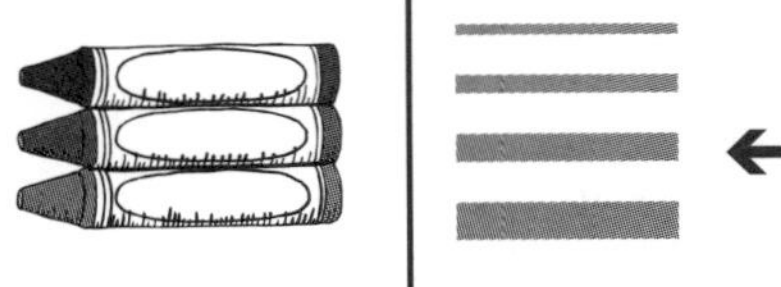

4 Choose the fill tool.

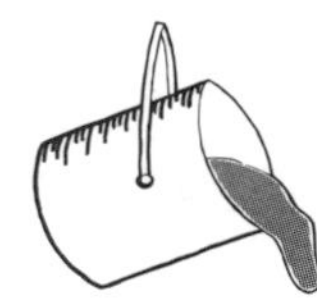

5 Color your drawing.

6 Draw a speech bubble.

7 Keyboard "Quack!" or "Quiet!" into the bubble.

8 Read the screen.

Rr

Read a Rainbow

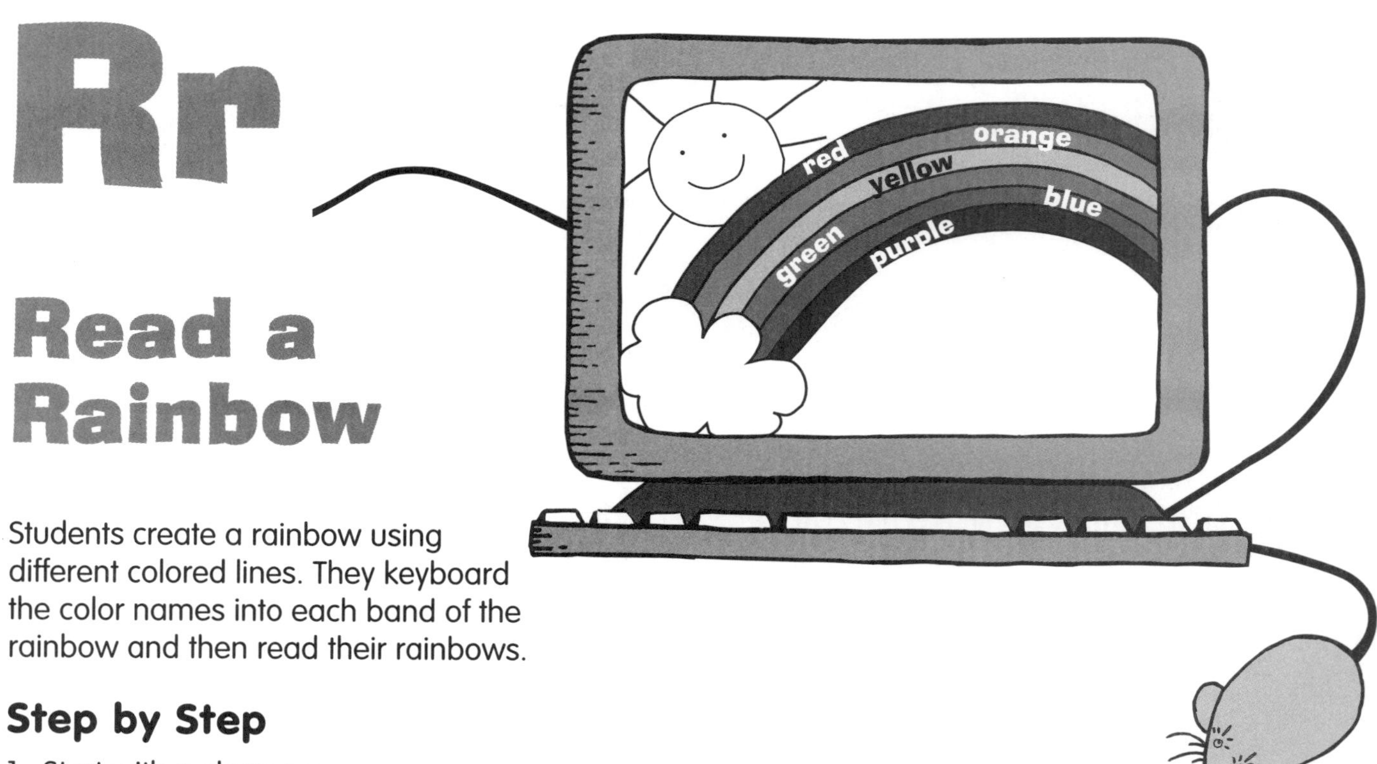

Students create a rainbow using different colored lines. They keyboard the color names into each band of the rainbow and then read their rainbows.

Step by Step

1. Start with a clean screen.
2. Choose the drawing tool and a thin line width.
3. Draw a little cloud with black.
4. Now pick a wide line width. Make a rainbow. Use the colors in order: red, orange, yellow, green, blue, and purple.
5. Choose the keyboard. Write the names of the colors.
6. Can you add a sun, too?
7. Read your rainbow.

Extending the Activity

- Have students stamp or draw objects that represent a color inside each line of the rainbow.
- Have students put a "treasure" at the end of the rainbow, then dictate a sentence about their treasure.

Literature Connections

Colors: How Do You Say It? by Meredith Dunham; Lothrop, Lee & Shepard Books, 1987.
The Gift of Driscoll Lipscomb by Sara Yamaka; Simon & Schuster Books for Young Readers, 1995.
How the Sky's Housekeeper Wore Her Scarves by Patricia Hooper; Little, Brown, 1995.
Is It red? Is It yellow? Is It blue? by Tana Hoban; Greenwillow Books, 1978.
John Burningham's Colors by John Burningham; Crown, 1986.
A Rainbow of My Own by Don Freemen; Viking Press, 1966.
Skyfire by Frank Asch; Prentice-Hall, 1984.

Read a Rainbow

1 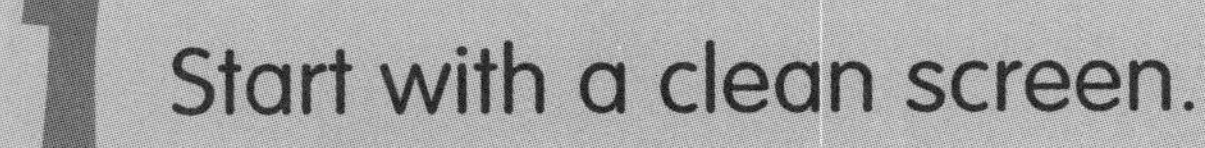
Start with a clean screen.

2 Choose the drawing tool and a thin line width.

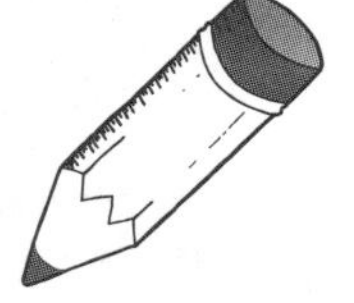

3 Draw a little cloud with black.

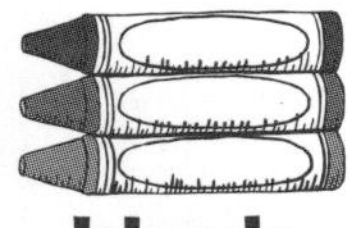

black

4 Now pick a wide line width.
Make a rainbow.
Use the colors in order:
red
orange
yellow
green
blue
purple

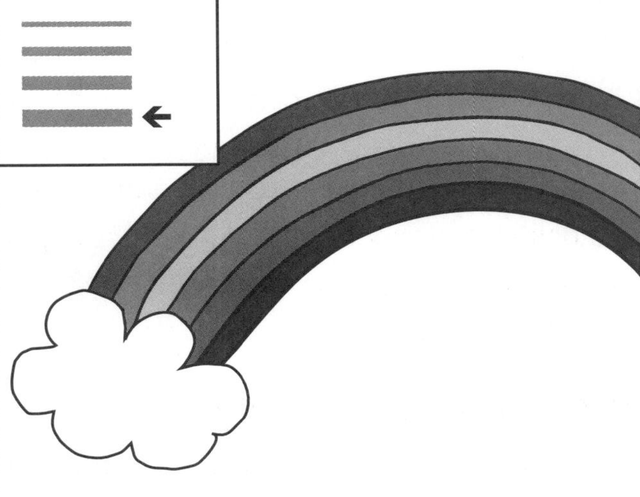

5 Choose the keyboard.
Write the names of the colors.

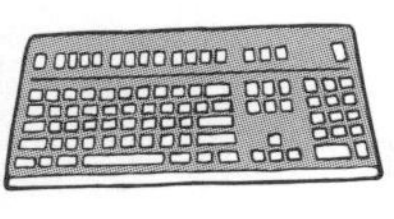

6 Can you add a sun, too?

7 Read your rainbow.

Ss

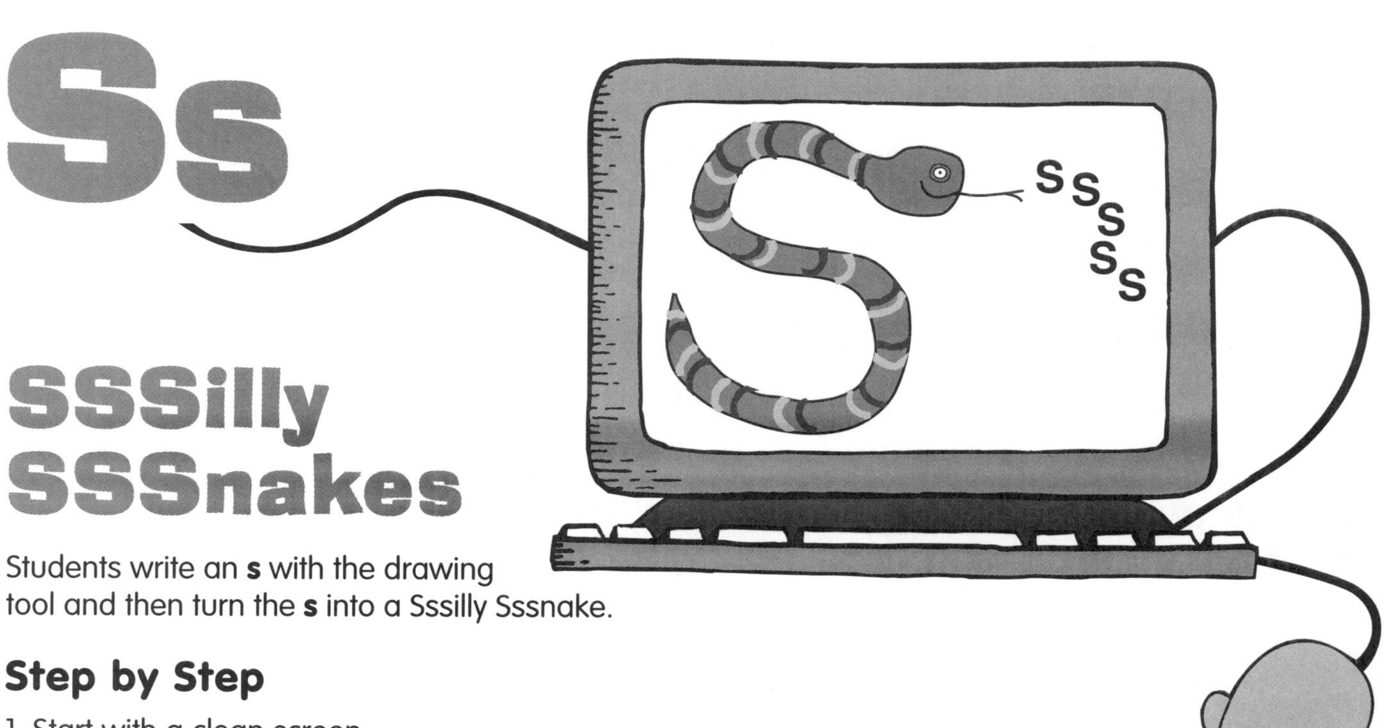

SSSilly SSSnakes

Students write an **s** with the drawing tool and then turn the **s** into a Sssilly Sssnake.

Step by Step

1. Start with a clean screen.
2. Choose the drawing tool, a color, and a line width.
3. Draw an **s** and turn it into a big snake.
4. Choose the fill tool and a color.
5. Color the body.
6. Choose the drawing tool, a color, and a line width.
7. Add stripes, dots, and a face.
8. Pick the letter stamp **s**. Add ssssss.
9. Print the page.

Extending the Activity

- Bind the pictures together in a class snake book. Students will love "reading" the hissing noise that the snakes make. As a class, write a story about a snake. Add the story to the pages of the book.
- Cut out the snakes. Staple the cutouts to a giant **s** and post on your wall.

Literature Connections

King Snake by Wendy Slotboom; Houghton Mifflin Co., 1997.
Snake Hunt by Jill Kastner; Four Winds Press, 1993.
The Snake: a Very Long Story by Bernard Waber; Houghton Mifflin, 1978.
Verdi by Janell Cannon; Harcourt Brace, 1997.
What's in the Cave? by Peter Seymour; Holt, Rinehart and Winston, 1985.

SSSilly SSSnakes

1 Start with a clean screen.

2 Choose the drawing tool, a color, and a line width.

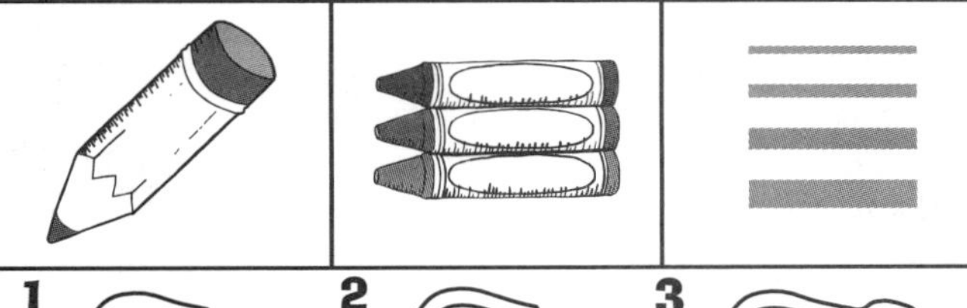

3 Draw an **s** and turn it into a big snake.

1 2 3

4 Choose the fill tool and a color.

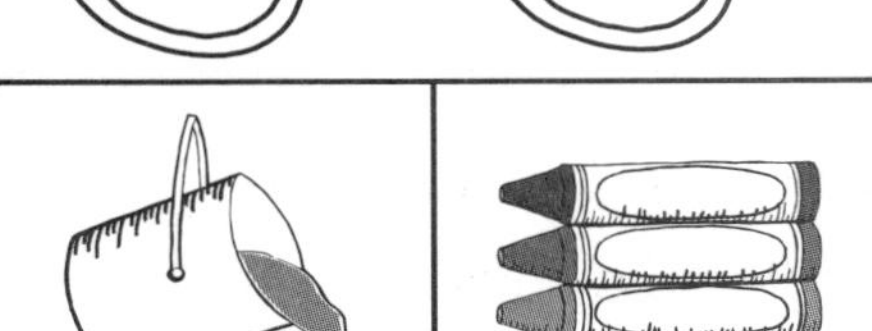

5 Color the body.

6 Choose the drawing tool, a color, and a line width.

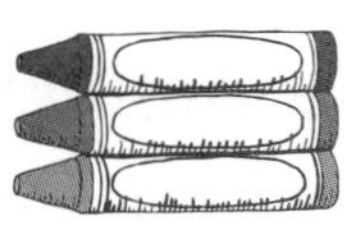

7 Add stripes, dots, and a face.

8 Pick the letter stamp **s**. Add ssssss.

ssssss

9 Print the page.

Tt

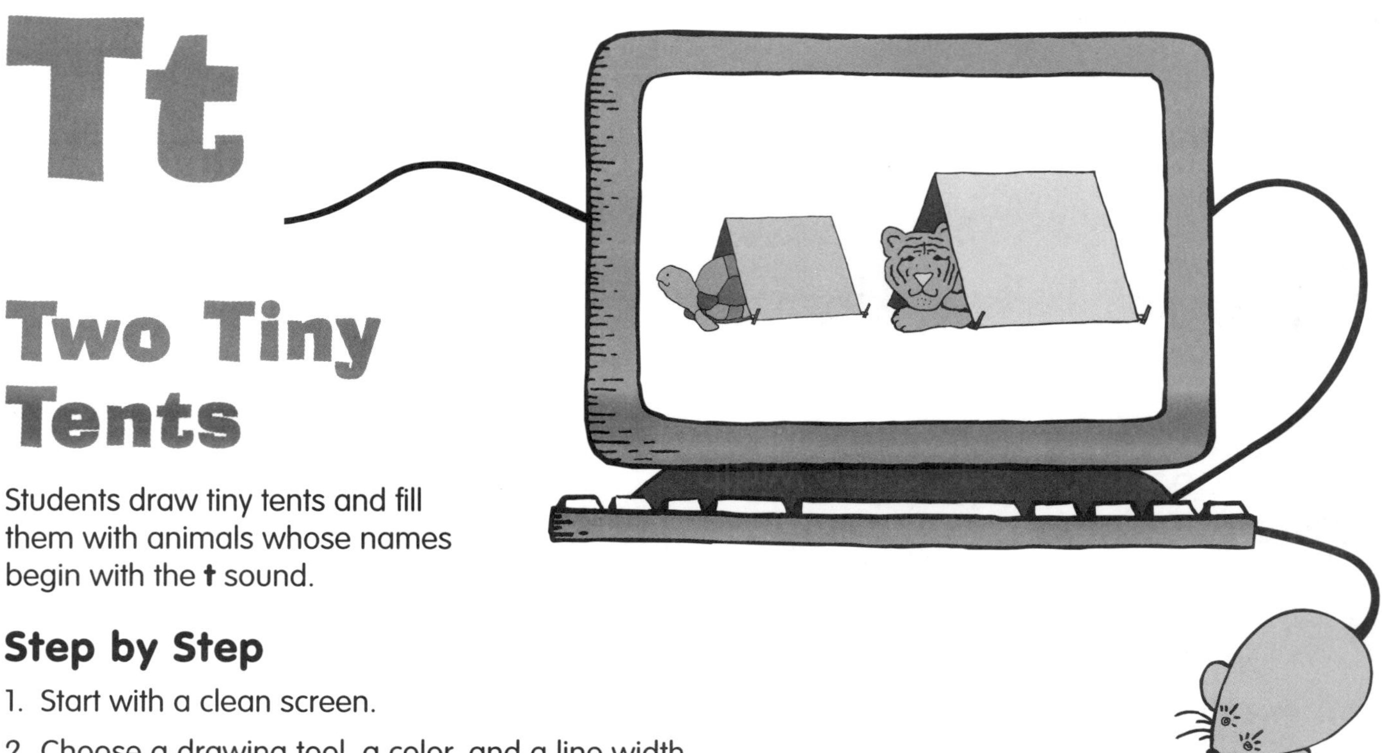

Two Tiny Tents

Students draw tiny tents and fill them with animals whose names begin with the **t** sound.

Step by Step

1. Start with a clean screen.
2. Choose a drawing tool, a color, and a line width.
3. Draw a tent.
4. Copy and paste the tent.
5. Choose the fill tool and a color. Color the tents.
6. Choose a drawing tool, a color, and a line width.
7. Draw an animal that begins with the **t** sound in each tent.
8. Choose the fill tool and color the animals.
9. Print the page.

Extending the Activity

- Have students keyboard the letter **t** on the outside of the tent before printing it. Cut out the tent and tape it to a craft stick. Students use the tent stick to signal when they hear a word that begins or ends with the **t** sound.
- Write a story about a tiny tent that follows the pattern of *The Mitten*. (Many versions are available.) Have students "fill" the tent with assorted animals until it bursts.

Literature Connections

Camping Out: A Book of Action Words by Betsy & Guillio Maestro; Crown, 1985.
Do Not Disturb by Nancy Tafuri; Greenwillow Books, 1987.
Starry Night by David Spohn; Lothrop, Lee & Shepard Books, 1992.
When Daddy Took Us Camping by Julie Brillhart; A. Whitman & Company, 1997.
When I Go Camping with Grandma by Marion Dane Bauer; Bridgewater Books, 1995.

Two Tiny Tents

1. Start with a clean screen.

2. Choose a drawing tool, a color, and a line width.

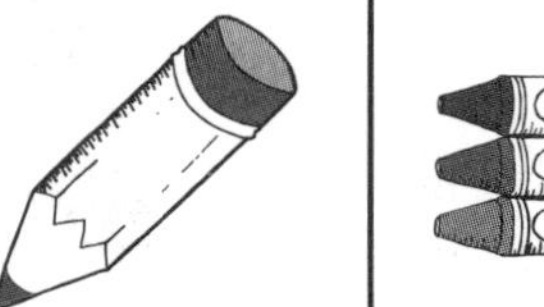
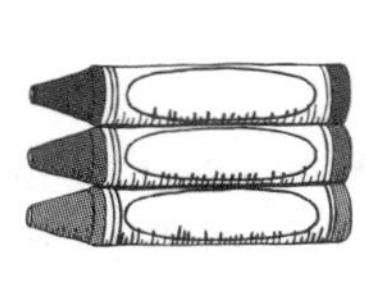

3. Draw a tent.

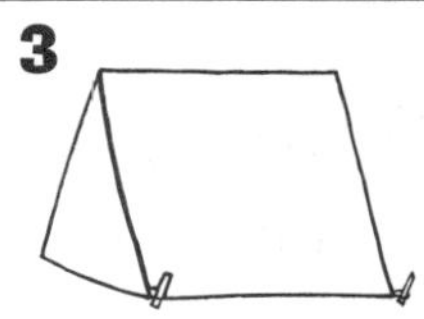

4. Copy and paste the tent.

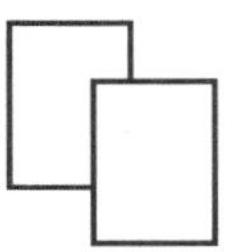

5. Choose the fill tool and a color. Color the tents.

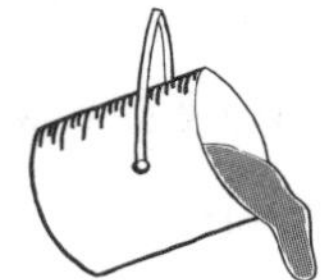
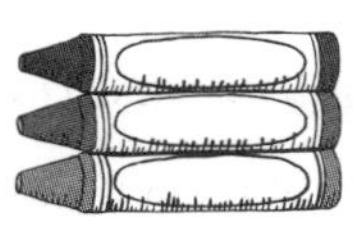
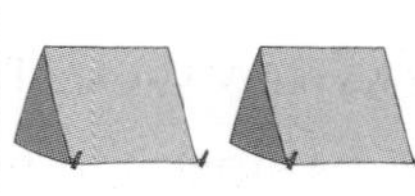

6. Choose a drawing tool, a color, and a line width.

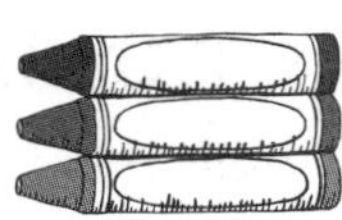

7. Draw an animal that begins with the **t** sound in each tent.

Tt

8. Choose the fill tool and color the animals.

9. Print the page.

Uu

Under an Umbrella

Students draw and decorate an umbrella with boots sticking out below.

Step by Step

1. Start with a clean screen.
2. Choose the drawing tool, a line width, and a color.
3. Draw a big umbrella.
4. Choose the fill tool and a color.
5. Color the umbrella.
6. Choose the drawing tool, a line width, and a color.
7. Draw two big boots under the umbrella.
8. Choose the fill tool and a color. Color the boots.
9. Print the page.

Extending the Activity

- On a second piece of paper, have students draw something that might be hiding under an umbrella. Ask them to tell about what's under the umbrella. Keyboard the sentence at the bottom of the second page. Mount the umbrella on top of the picture.
- Read the poem, "The Umbrella Brigade" (*The Sound of Poetry* by Mary C. Austin and Queenie B. Mills; Allyn and Bacon, 1967) to your class. March around the room as you repeat the refrain.

Literature Connections

Henry & Mudge in Puddle Trouble by Cynthia Rylant; Bradbury Press, 1987.
Peter Spier's Rain by Peter Spier; Doubleday, 1982.
Rain Drop Splash by Alvin Tresselt; Lothrop, Lee & Shepard Co., 1946.
The Umbrella Day by Nancy Evan Cooney; Philomel Books, 1989.
Umbrella by Taro Yashima; Viking Press, 1958.

Under an Umbrella

1	Start with a clean screen.	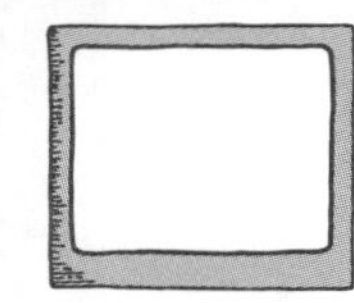		
2	Choose the drawing tool, a line width, and a color.	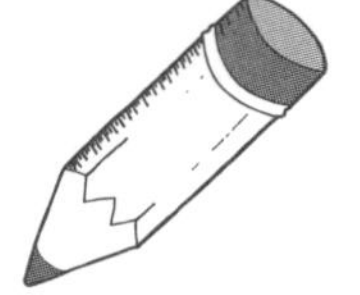		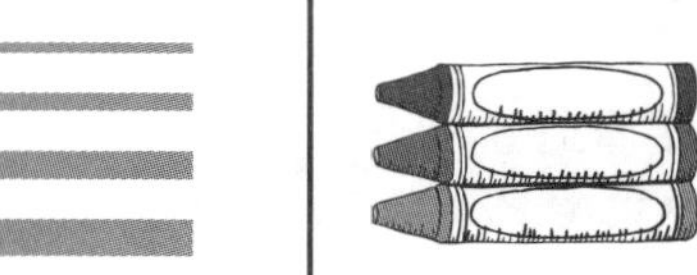
3	Draw a big umbrella.	 1	 2	
4	Choose the fill tool and a color.		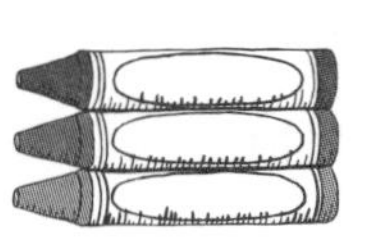	
5	Color the umbrella.			
6	Choose the drawing tool, a line width, and a color.	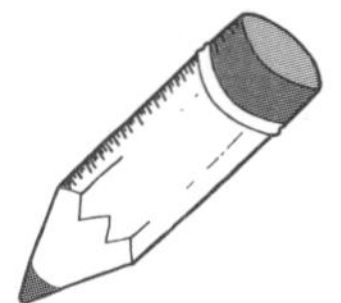		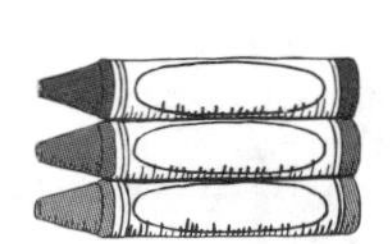
7	Draw two big boots under the umbrella.			
8	Choose the fill tool and a color. Color the boots.	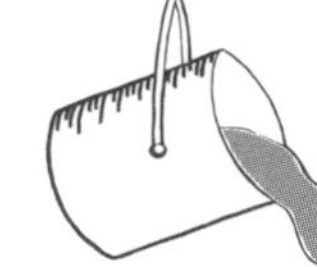	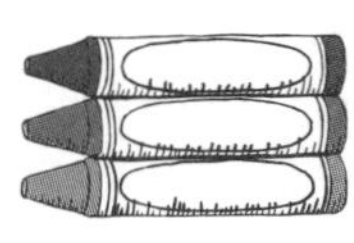	
9	Print the page.			

Vv

A Vase of Very Violet Violets

Students will create a picture by cutting and pasting a vase of violets.

Step by Step

1. Start with a clean screen.
2. Choose the rectangle tool and a textured color.
3. Make a rectangle.
4. Choose the drawing tool, a solid color, and a line width.
5. Draw a vase with violets.
6. Choose the fill tool and the color violet.
7. Fill the flowers.
8. Copy and paste some vases.
9. Print the page.

Extending the Activity

Mount the printed picture on a piece of colored construction paper. Paste the mounted picture to a folded piece of construction paper to create a card for a special occasion.

Literature Connections

Rosy's Garden by Elizabeth Laird; Philomel Books, 1990.
Planting a Rainbow by Lois Ehlert; Harcourt Brace, 1988.
The Rose in My Garden by Arnold Lobel; Greenwillow Books, 1984.

A Vase of Very Violet Violets

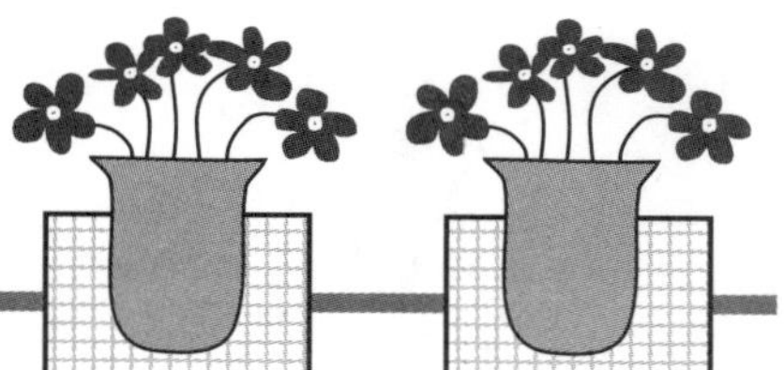

1	Start with a clean screen.			
2	Choose the rectangle tool and a textured color.	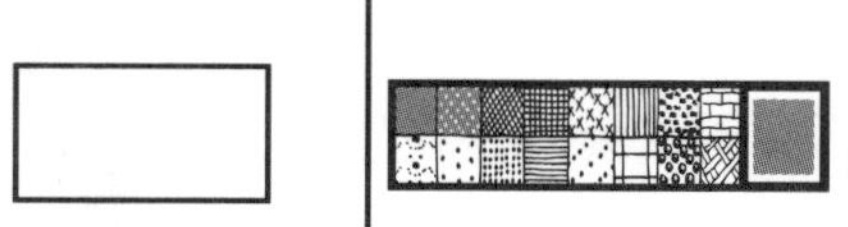		
3	Make a rectangle.	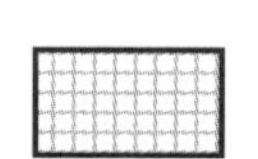		
4	Choose the drawing tool, a solid color, and a line width.	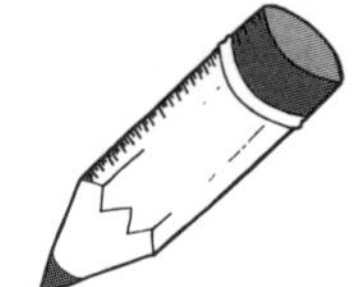	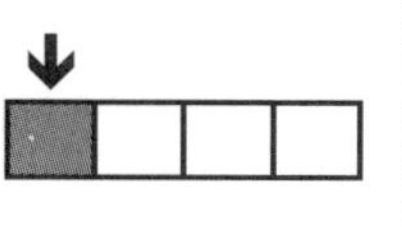	
5	Draw a vase with violets.	1 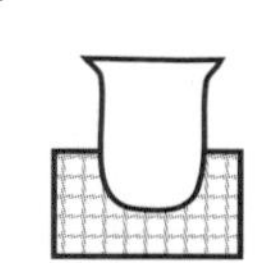	2 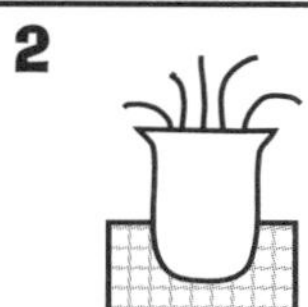	3 
6	Choose the fill tool and the color violet.	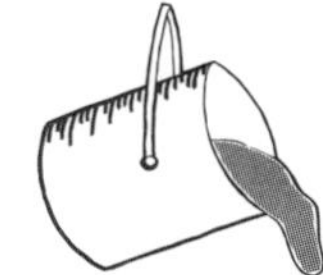	 violet	
7	Fill the flowers.			
8	Copy and paste some vases.	**select**	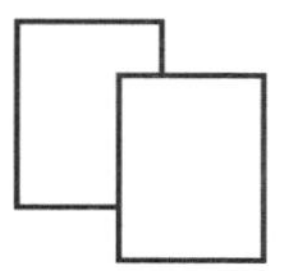	
9	Print the page.			

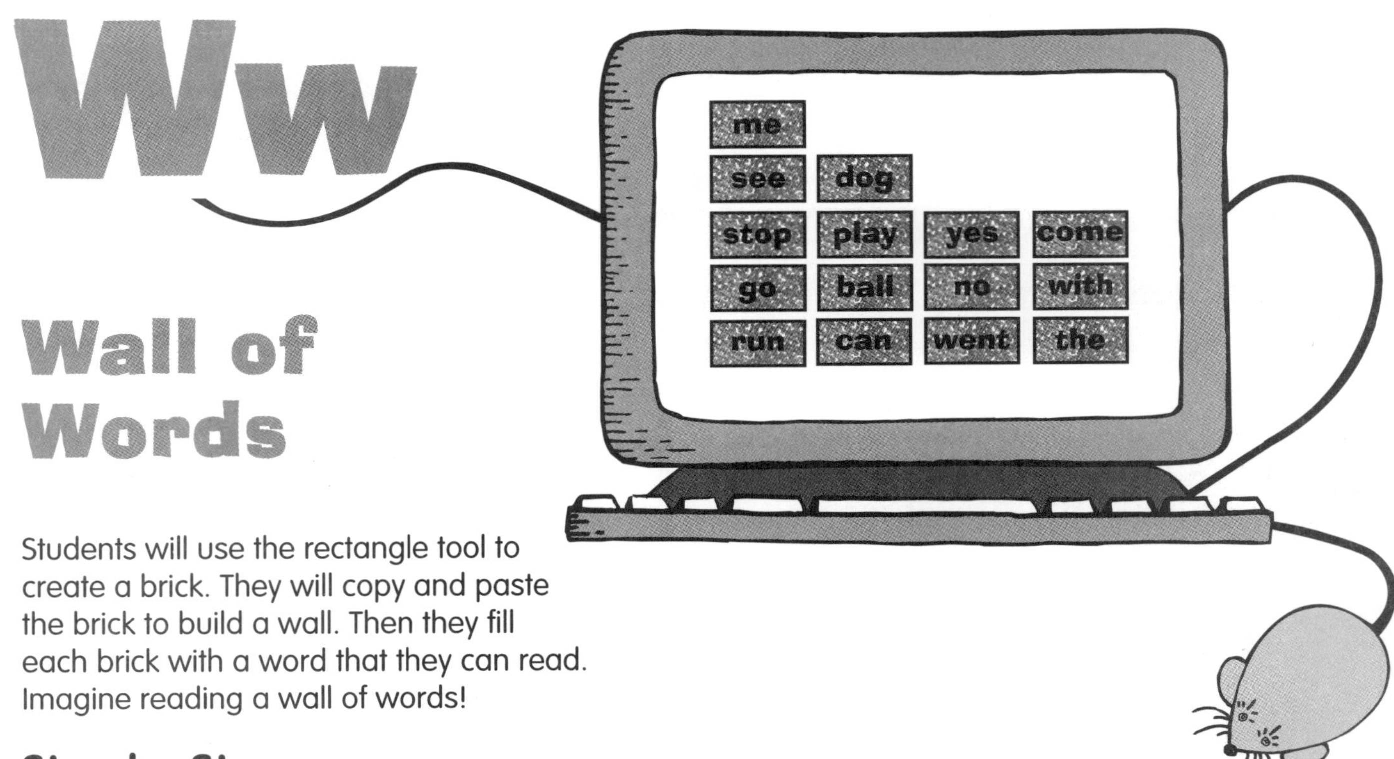

Wall of Words

Students will use the rectangle tool to create a brick. They will copy and paste the brick to build a wall. Then they fill each brick with a word that they can read. Imagine reading a wall of words!

Step by Step

1. Start with a clean screen.
2. Choose a rectangle tool, a color, and a texture.
3. Make a brick.
4. Copy the brick and paste it again and again to make a wall.
5. Choose the keyboard.
6. Type a word in each brick.
7. Print the page.
8. Read the wall.

Extending the Activity

- Create a classroom wall of words. Make a larger rectangular brick using the rectangle tool. Save the brick as a template. Add words to the bricks, print, and mount on the wall. Soon you will have a tall wall.
- Change the activity by asking students to draw a picture of something that begins with the **w** sound on each brick.

Literature Connections

The Greatest of All retold by Eric A. Kimmel; Holiday House, 1991.
Matthew Wheelock's Wall by Frances Ward Weller; Macmillan, 1992.
Tillie & the Wall by Leo Lionni; Knopf, 1989.
What Is a Wall, After All? by Judy Allen; Candlewick Press, 1993.

Wall of Words

1	Start with a clean screen.			
2	Choose a rectangle tool, a color, and a texture.	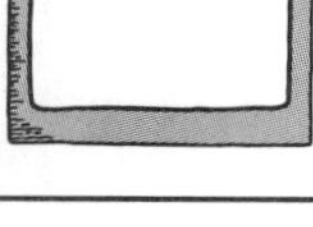	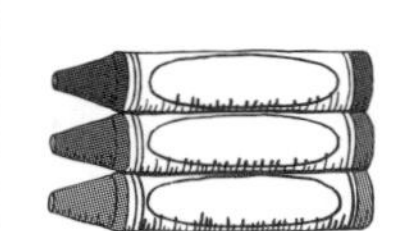	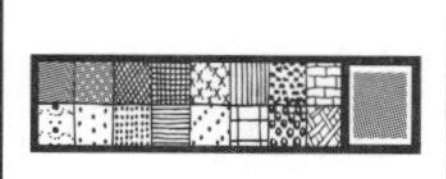
3	Make a brick.	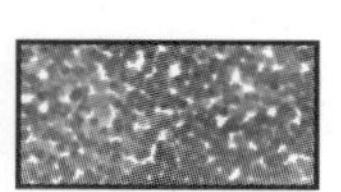		
4	Copy the brick and paste it again and again to make a wall.	 select	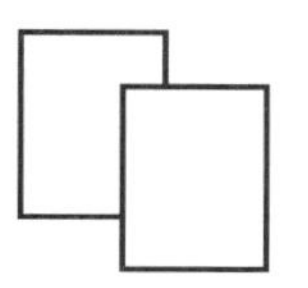	 Paste
5	Choose the keyboard.	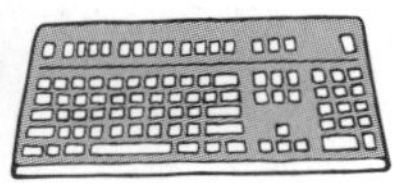		
6	Type a word in each brick.	 see		
7	Print the page.			
8	Read the wall.			

Xx
X Marks the Spot!

Students work in pairs and play tic-tac-toe.

Step by Step

1. Start with a clean screen.
2. Choose the line tool.
3. Draw a tic-tac-toe grid.
4. Choose the letter stamps.
5. One person uses **X**. The other person uses **O**.
6. Take turns putting your stamps on the grid.
7. Three in a row wins.

Extending the Activity

Teach your students other traditional paper/pencil games. Work on the computer instead of using paper.

Pen the Pig

1. Create a template of dots in a grid.
2. Students choose the line tool and connect two dots. When a student completes the fourth side of a square, he or she claim the "pen." They could use a stamp or an initial for labeling the pen.

Hang Man

1. Students use the drawing tools to draw blanks representing each letter of a word.
2. Other students guess letters in an attempt to discover the mystery word. If a guess is correct, the letter is stamped on the line. If the guess is incorrect, the letter is stamped at the bottom of the screen.
3. The drawing tool is used to draw the hangman's galley and add the hanging man. One part is added for each wrong guess.

Literature Connections

Ethan's Favorite Teacher by Hila Colman; Crown Publishers, 1975.(teacher's reference)
Pencil Paper Games by Karl-Heinz Koch; Sterling Publishing Co., 1991.
The Picture Rulebook of Kids' Games by Roxanne Henderson; Contemporary Books, 1996.

X Marks the Spot!

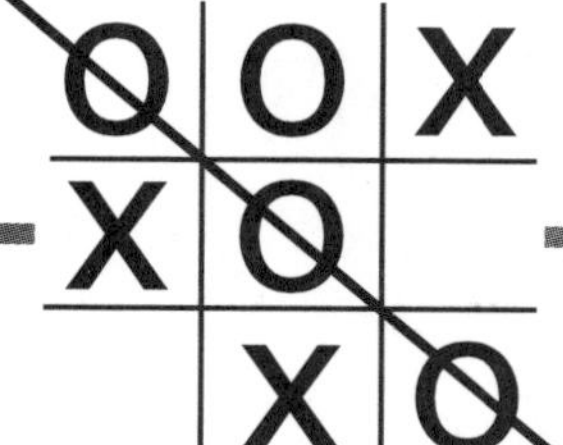

1	Start with a clean screen.	
2	Choose the line tool.	
3	Draw a tic-tac-toe grid.	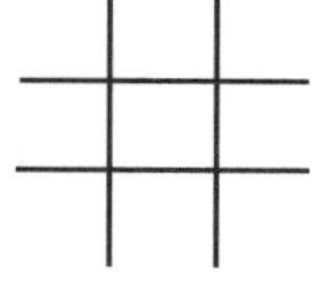
4	Choose the letter stamps.	
5	One person uses **X**. The other person uses **O**.	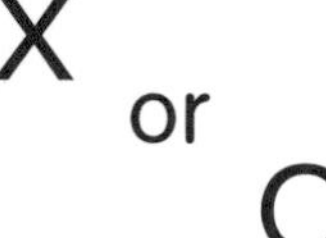
6	Take turns putting your stamps on the grid.	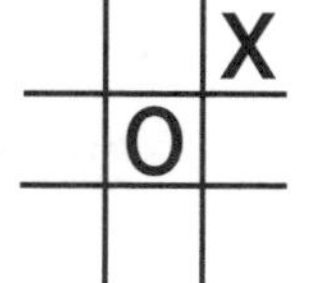
7	Three in a row wins.	

Yy

Yes, Yes, Yes!

Students draw a picture to represent a question/answer situation in which they would answer with the phrase "Yes, Yes, Yes!"

Step by Step

1. Start with a clean screen.
2. Choose the drawing tool, a line width, and a color.
3. Draw two people talking.
4. Add a speech bubble.
5. Choose the keyboard.
6. Type the words: Yes, Yes, Yes!
7. Print the page.

Extending the Activity

- Have an adult or cross-age tutor assist students in typing the questions that are being asked in each picture. Share the printed dialogues with the class. Have students read the "Yes, Yes, Yes!" lines.
- Have students divide their screens into two sections. Label one section "Yes" and one section "No." Have students stamp things that they like on the "yes" side and things that they don't like on the "no" side.

Literature Connections

If I Found a Wistful Unicorn by Ann Ashford; Peachtree Publishers, 1978.
Yes by Josse Goffin; Lothrop, Lee & Shepard, 1993.
Yo! Yes? by Chris Raschka; Scholastic, 1993.

Yes, Yes, Yes!

1 Start with a clean screen.

2 Choose the drawing tool, a line width, and a color.

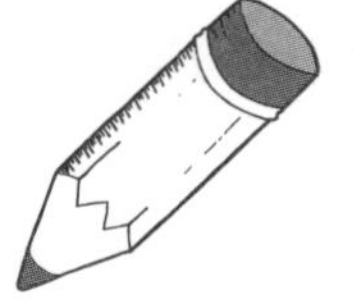

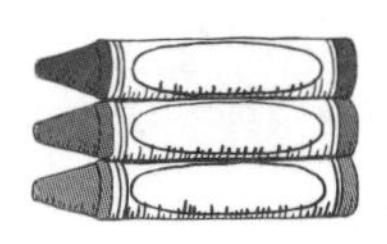

3 Draw two people talking.

4 Add a speech bubble.

5 Choose the keyboard.

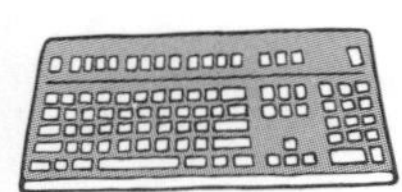

6 Type the words: Yes, Yes, Yes!

7 Print the page.

Zz

Zebra in a Zigzag Zoo

Students draw a zebra and then give the animal a zany zigzag cage.

Step by Step

1. Start with a clean screen.
2. Choose the drawing tool and a line width.
3. Pick the color black.
4. Draw a zebra.
5. Make black stripes.
6. Add a face, a mane, and a tail.
7. Choose the line tool.
8. Make a zigzag cage.
9. Print the page.

Extending the Activity

- Mount the zebras on black construction paper and hang them on a bulletin board to create a Zany Zebra Zoo.
- Give the zebras names and label them. Using two index cards labeled "Start" and "Finish," mark two cages. Then practice giving and following oral directions. For example:

  "Tell me how to get from Zero's cage to Zack's cage."
  "Turn right and go by three cages. Then turn left. Go past two more cages, and you will be at Zack's cage."

Literature Connections

At the Zoo by Douglas Florian; Greenwillow Books, 1992.
The Baby Zoo by Bruce McMillan; Scholastic Inc., 1992.
A Children's Zoo by Tana Hoban; Greenwillow Books, 1985.
If Anything Ever Goes Wrong at the Zoo by Mary Jean Hendrick; Harcourt Brace Jovanovich, 1993.
What Would You Do If You Lived At The Zoo? by Nancy White Carlstrom; Little, Brown, 1994.
When We Went to the Zoo by Jan Ormerod; Lothrop, Lee & Shepard, 1991.
Zoo Dreams by Cor Hazelaar; Frances Foster Books, 1997.
Zoo-looking by Mem Fox; Mondo Pub., 1996.

Zebra in a Zigzag Zoo

1 Start with a clean screen.

2 Choose the drawing tool and a line width.

3 Pick the color black.

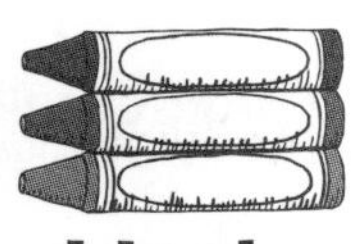

4 Draw a zebra.

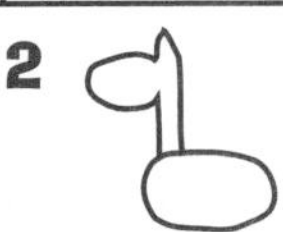

5 Make black stripes.

6 Add a face, a mane, and a tail.

7 Choose the line tool.

8 Make a zigzag cage.

9 Print the page.

What's Its Sound?

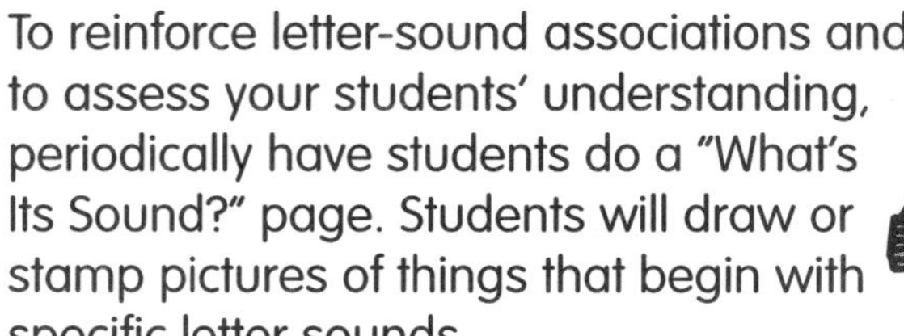
To reinforce letter-sound associations and to assess your students' understanding, periodically have students do a "What's Its Sound?" page. Students will draw or stamp pictures of things that begin with specific letter sounds.

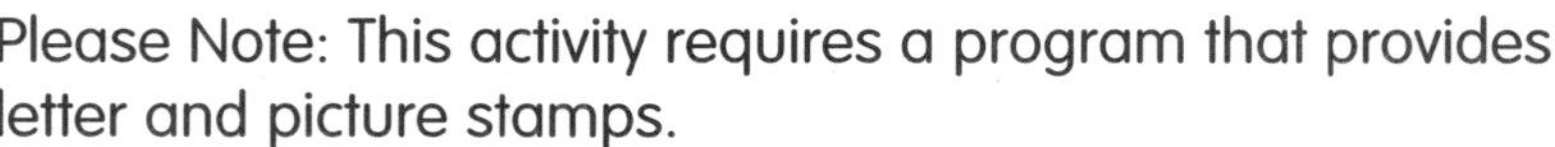
Please Note: This activity requires a program that provides letter and picture stamps.

Step by Step

1. Start with a clean screen.
2. Choose the letter stamp.
3. Stamp the letters__________. Spread them out.
4. Choose the picture stamp.
5. Look at the stamps. Say the name of each picture.
6. Find a picture that begins with a letter you stamped.
7. Stamp the picture by the letter.
8. Find a picture for each letter.
9. Print the page.

Hint: You may begin the lesson with a template instead of having students put their own letters on their pages. (See page 4 for making templates.) If you use a template, student directions begin with step 4.

What's Its Sound?

1 Start with a clean screen.

2 Choose the letter stamp.

3 Stamp the letters______.
Spread them out.

M C D S

4 Choose the picture stamp.

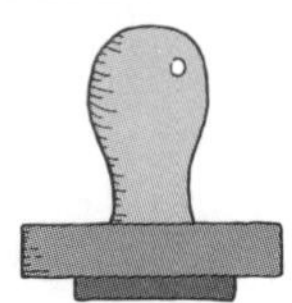

5 Look at the stamps.
Say the name of each picture.

6 Find a picture that begins with a letter you stamped.

7 Stamp the picture by the letter.

8 Find a picture for each letter.

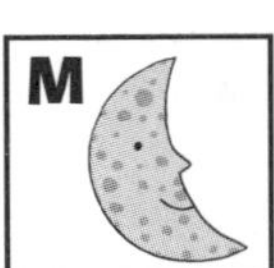

9 Print the page.

Chicka Chicka Boom Boom

Bill Martin Jr.'s and John Archambault's bright and bold book, *Chicka Chicka Boom Boom*, is a great starting point for a beginning lesson in alphabetical order.

Step by Step

1. Start with a clean screen.
2. Choose the drawing tool, a color, and a line width.
3. Draw a coconut tree.
4. Choose the letter stamp.
5. Click on the letter **A**.
6. Move the **A** up and down.
7. Stamp the **A** at the top of the page.
8. Repeat with every letter.
9. Print the page.

Literature Connection

Chicka Chicka Boom Boom by Bill Martin Jr. & John Archambault; Simon & Schuster Books for Young Readers, 1989.

Chicka Chicka Boom Boom

A B C D E F G H I J K L M
N O P Q R S T U V W X Y Z

1 Start with a clean screen.

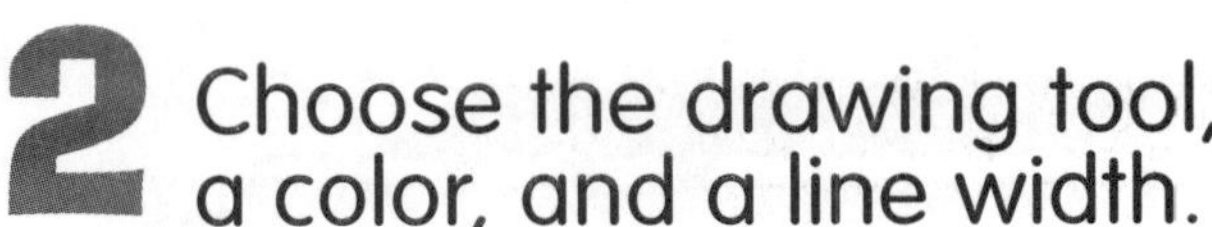

2 Choose the drawing tool, a color, and a line width.

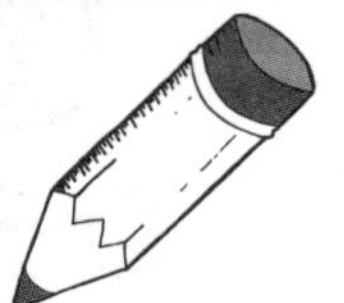

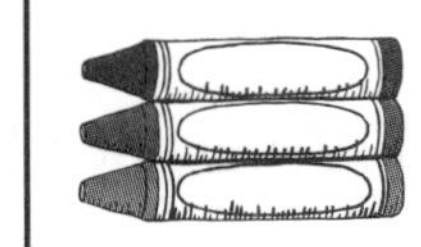

3 Draw a coconut tree.

1 

2 

3 

4 Choose the letter stamp.

5 Click on the letter **A**.

6 Move the **A** up and down the coconut tree.

7 Stamp the **A** at the top of the page.

A
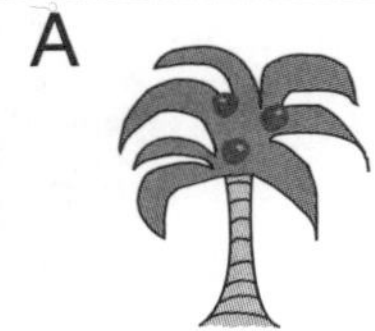

8 Repeat with every letter.

A B C D E F G H I J K L M
N O P Q R S T U V W X Y Z

9 Print the page.

Alphabet Soup

Students fill a bowl with letters and then match the letters with pictures showing that they know letter sounds.

Step by Step

1. Start with a clean screen.
2. Choose the drawing tool, a color, and a line width.
3. Draw a big bowl.
4. Choose the letter stamps.
5. Stamp four letters in the bowl.
6. Choose the picture stamps.
7. Stamp pictures that begin with each letter in the bowl.
8. Print the page.

Extensions

- Students use only one letter, stamping it several times in the bowl and then fill the bowl with pictures of things that begin with that letter.
- Draw a giant bowl on the chalkboard. Assign each student a letter of the alphabet. On the computer, students write the letter and draw or stamp one or two things that begin with the letter. Print the pictures and post them in the bowl.

Literature Connections

Alphabet Soup by Kate Banks; Knopf, 1988.
Alphabet Soup by Scott Gustofson; Contemporary Books, 1990.
Martha Blah Blah by Susan Meddaugh; Houghton Mifflin, 1996.
Martha Speaks by Susan Meddaugh; Houghton Mifflin, 1992.

Alphabet Soup

1 Start with a clean screen.

2 Choose the drawing tool, a color, and a line width.

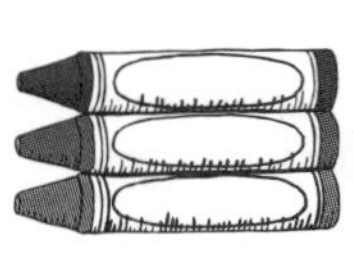

3 Draw a big bowl.

4 Choose the letter stamps.

5 Stamp four letters in the bowl.

6 Choose the picture stamps.

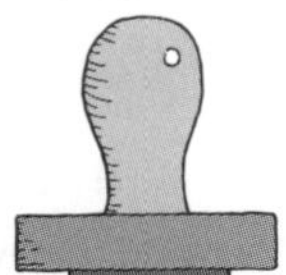

7 Stamp pictures that begin with each letter in the bowl.

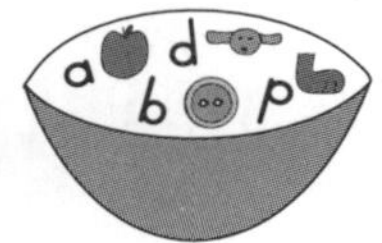

8 Print the page.

Alphabet Book

Students love to read the books that they create. Make an alphabet book for your classroom. Assign each student one letter and have them create a page showing that letter and an illustration that begins with the letter sound.

Step by Step

1. Start with a clean screen.
2. Choose the drawing tool, a color, and a line width.
3. Write a letter.
4. Draw a picture of something that begins with the letter.
5. Choose the fill tool.
6. Color the picture.
7. Add details with the drawing tool.
8. Print the page.

Extensions

- Add a sentence to each page.

  B is for Bobby who bounces a ball.

- Create an alphabet theme book. For example, if you are learning about farms, make a farm alphabet book so that each letter stands for something on the farm.

Literature Connections

Read several of the wonderful alphabet books you find in your school or public library.

Alphabet Book

1 Start with a clean screen.

2 Choose the drawing tool, a color, and a line width.

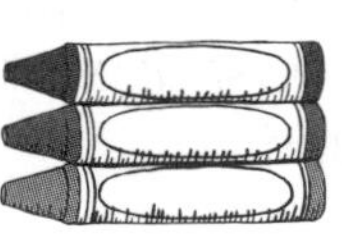

3 Write a letter.

M

4 Draw a picture of something that begins with the letter.

5 Choose the fill tool.

6 Color the picture.

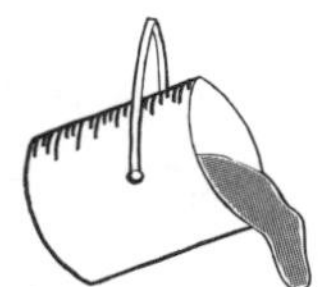

7 Add details with the drawing tool.

8 Print the page.

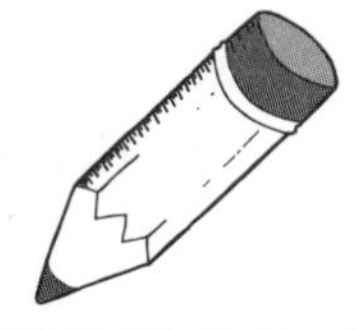

Alphabet Parade

Let your students become part of the alphabet. Create giant letter cards for students to hold as they march in an alphabet parade.

Step by Step

1. Start with a clean screen.
2. Choose the drawing tool, a color, and a wide line width.
3. Hold down the shift key. Use the mouse to pull lines to make a box.
4. Draw the letter in the middle. Make it big.
5. Choose the fill tool and a color.
6. Color the letter.
7. Choose the picture stamps. Find a stamp that begins with the letter sound.
8. Print the letter card.

Before the parade, paste the cards to pieces of cardboard. Make your parade as simple or as elaborate as you want. Marchers can simply carry the letter cards or they might also carry objects that start with that letter. They could dress up representing activities that start with each letter.

Extensions

- Laminate the letter cards. Have students put them in alphabetical order.
- Display some or all of the letter cards, showing an object. Have students choose the card that stands for the letter at the beginning of the object's name.

Literature Connections

The Alphabet Parade by Seymour Chwast; Harcourt Brace Jovanovich, 1991.
Animal Parade by Jakki Wood; Bradbury Press, 1993.
Fiddle-i-fee: A Farmyard Song for the Very Young adapted by Melissa Sweet; Little, Brown, 1992.
One Bear, One Dog by Paul Strickland; Dutton Children's Books, 1997.

Alphabet Parade

1 Start with a clean screen.

2 Choose the drawing tool,
a color, and a wide line width.

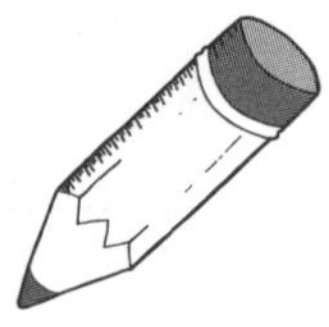
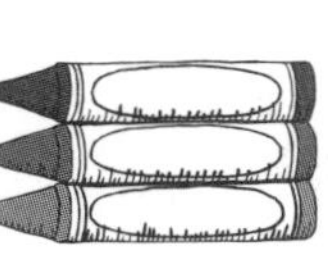

3 Hold down the shift key.
Use the mouse to pull a line.

4 Draw the letter in the middle.
Make it big.

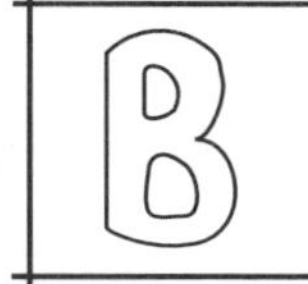

5 Choose the fill tool and
a color.

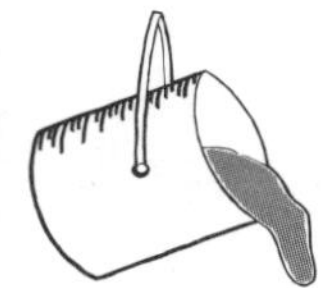
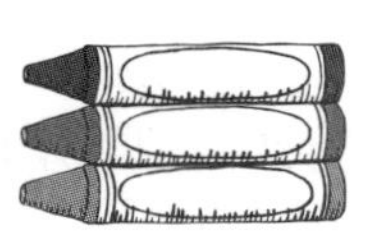

6 Color the letter.

7 Choose the picture stamps.
What begins with that sound?

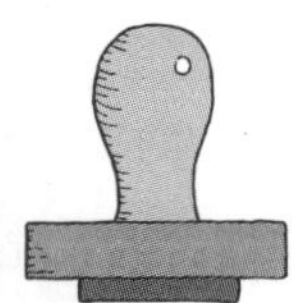

8 Print the letter card.

Checklist of Computer Skills

Teaching and Learning with the Computer Student Names	Identify computer parts	Open hard drive	Open programs	Click mouse	Double-click mouse	Point	Drag	Draw	Choose tool	Fill with color	Respect and care for computers

Checklist of Projects

Teaching and Learning with the Computer

Individual-Letter Activities														
A Row of Apples														
Big Brown Bear														
Catch a Colorful Caterpillar														
Delightful Dinosaurs														
Easy Eggs														
Fancy Fish														
A Gaggle of Geese														
Hats, Hats, Hats														
Incredible Insects														
Just Jellyfish														
Kites														
Lovely Lavender Lines														
Musical Mice														
Nifty Nests														
No Ordinary Octopus														
Purple Pockets														
Quack, Quack, Quiet														
Read a Rainbow														
Sssilly Sssnakes														
Two Tiny Tents														
Under an Umbrella														
A Vase of Very Violet Violets														
Wall of Words														
X Marks the Spot!														
Yes, Yes, Yes!														
Zebra in a Zigzag Zoo														
Multiple-Letter Activities														
What's Its Sound?														
Chicka Chicka Boom Boom														
Alphabet Soup														
Alphabet Book														
Alphabet Parade														

A B C D E F G H

Dear Parents,

Here is an alphabet project that your child completed on the computer.

Using the computer as a tool for learning is an important part of our curriculum. Many of the reading and writing skills that your child is learning will be practiced and reinforced by doing activities on the computer. At the same time, your child will be increasing his or her level of computer literacy.

Ask your child to tell you about how this project was done and what he or she knows about the letter practiced, for example:

- What is the name of the letter?
- What sound does the letter make?
- Can you name three other things that begin with the letter?
- Can you show me how to write the letter?

Thank you for your help and your interest in the language and computer skills your child is learning this year.

Sincerely,

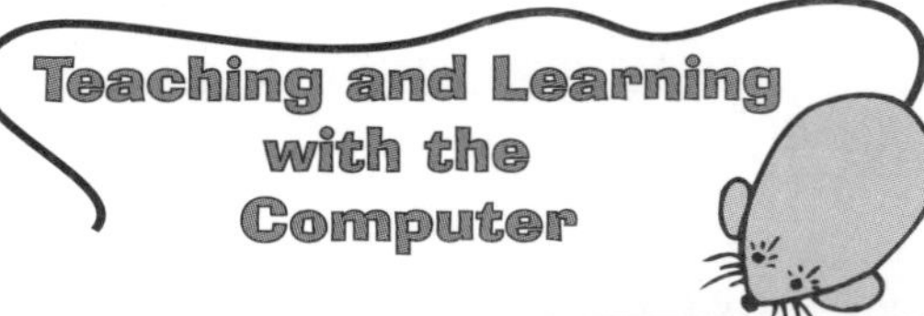

A B C D E F G H

Dear Parents,

Here is an alphabet project that your child completed on the computer.

Using the computer as a tool for learning is an important part of our curriculum. Many of the reading and writing skills that your child is learning will be practiced and reinforced by doing activities on the computer. At the same time, your child will be increasing his or her level of computer literacy.

Ask your child to tell you about how this project was done and what he or she knows about the letter practiced, for example:

- What is the name of the letter?
- What sound does the letter make?
- Can you name three other things that begin with the letter?
- Can you show me how to write the letter?

Thank you for your help and your interest in the language and computer skills your child is learning this year.

Sincerely,

Teaching and Learning
with the
Computer